The Critical Idiom

Founder Editor: John D. Jump 1969-76

40   *Comedy of Manners*

In the same series

Comedy of Manners/

David L. Hirst

Methuen & Co Ltd

First published 1979
by Methuen & Co Ltd
11 New Fetter Lane, London EC4P 4EE

© 1979 David L. Hirst

Typset by Inforum Ltd, Portsmouth
Printed in Great Britain by
J.W. Arrowsmith Ltd, Bristol 3

ISBN 0 416 85590 3 (hardbound)
ISBN 0 416 85570 9 (paperback)

Contents

For TONY

Acknowledgements

I must thank Robin Allanson and Tadeusz Karolak whose generosity and hospitality made this book much easier to write; and Pat Davis who kindly typed the final version.

1

Introduction

> 'You must beware of thinking too much about style', said my kindly
> adviser, 'or you will become like those fastidious people who polish
> and polish until there is nothing left.'
> 'Then there really are such people?' I asked eagerly. But the well-
> informed lady could give me no precise information about them. I
> often hear of them in this tantalising manner, and perhaps one of
> these days I shall have the luck to come across them.
>
> (Logan Pearsall Smith, Preface to *All Trivia*, 1933)

When John Osborne called his play *The End of me Old Cigar*
(1975) 'a modern comedy of modern manners' he drew attention to the fact that this genre of comedy, which dominated the
immediate post-Restoration period, has continued as a vital
aspect of English theatre to the present day. One can trace a
line of development from the playwrights of the second half of
the seventeenth century through Sheridan and Goldsmith in
the eighteenth, W.S. Gilbert and Wilde in the nineteenth to the
inter-war comedies of Maugham, Coward and Lonsdale.
More recently Orton, Pinter and Osborne have achieved a
more marked dramatic precision by adopting the features of
this comic mode.

The subject of comedy of manners is the way people behave,
the manners they employ in a social context; the chief concerns
of the characters are sex and money (and thus the interrelated
topics of marriage, adultery and divorce); the style is distinguished by the refinement of raw emotional expression and
action in the subtlety of wit and intrigue. The comedy of man-

ners is at its most expressive when all three of these aspects interact. But it is possible to have one without the others: Sheridan, for example, is all superficial style; Coward's *Hay Fever* is a perfect comedy of manners in its subject, but it has no concern with money and is far less witty than his finest works. Style is all-important in these plays. By style is meant not merely a superficial manner of expression but a definition of behaviour. The winners are always those with the most style: the sharpest wits, the subtlest intriguers. This has led to the repeated charge that the comedy of manners is immoral and unpleasant. It is undoubtedly the most anti-romantic form of comedy, for in plays of this type the conventional moral standards are superseded by the criterion of taste, of what constitutes 'good form'.

Orton's *Loot* ends with the observation: 'People would talk; we must keep up appearances', a belief basic not only to his plays but to the genre as a whole. Such a comment is an echo of Pope's satiric lines in 'The Rape of the Lock' where Belinda regrets:

'Oh hadst thou, cruel, been content to seize
Hairs less in sight, or any hairs but these!'
    (Pope, 'The Rape of the Lock', IV, 4. ll. 175-6)

Actions — rape, robbery, murder, adultery — are unimportant; what matters is the way in which they are performed, or more often the style with which they are concealed. Whether it be the careful euphemisms Orton's characters employ, the wit of Mirabel and Millamant, the clipped tones of Elyot and Amanda, or the epigrams of Wilde's exquisitely refined ladies and gentlemen, the keynote of these plays is decorum. This has given rise to another criticism: that of a shallowness and lack of sincerity in the characters and their authors. The unscrupulous sexual and monetary acquisitiveness of these figures may initially seem at sharp variance with their refinement of speech, though it is not merely their actions, but, more importantly, the manner in which these characters conduct themselves that secures their victory. They are playing a game, perhaps, but in deadly earnest and for the highest of stakes; and, moreover, they must stick to the rules. These rules are society's unwritten laws regulating behaviour, the dictates of propriety which, though they may differ in detail from age to age and class to class, are always basic to the conduct of the characters in the comedy of manners.

It is a dramatic genre that is particularly closely related to the social conditions of the time. A careful examination of the periods in which this type of comedy has flourished in England reveals that high style and fashion in every case distinguished the behaviour of society. The Restoration era was the age of the beau and his imitator, the fop; dress and deportment continued to be important, though more restrained in the eighteenth century; but the drabness and heaviness of the Victorian period put an end to the love of and pride in being well-dressed. In reaction, Wilde and others at the end of the century found the need to flaunt their abhorrence of conventional taste in dress and behaviour. With Wilde the dandy was reborn, and this figure was to reappear in the inter-war period and again in the 1960s. Both the 'roaring', 'gay' 1920s and the age of *Hair* and Carnaby Street were periods in which fashion, and notably male fashion, asserted themselves, and it is precisely in these times that the comedy of manners, dormant throughout the drab, unstylish 1940s and 1950s as through the Victorian era, again became a significant comic genre. Critics of all these periods — from the late seventeenth century through to the 1960s — have accused this vogue for ostentatious male dress of decadence and effeminacy. The dandies have had their own disarming reply, which from Wilde to Osborne has been the same: that effeminacy always makes a man more attractive to women. Such witticisms also serve to mask another aspect of the comedy of manners; from the time of Wilde it has often been the province of homosexual writers: Wilde, Coward,

Maugham and Orton all translated their life-style into their plays, whilst the nature of homosexual relationships features repeatedly in the work of Pinter and Osborne.

Since the beau and the dandy in all these periods sets himself up as the arbiter of good taste, not only in dress but in behaviour, he acts as a powerful critic of conventional values. As Felstiner put it in *The Lies of Art*, 'A figure of the counter-culture, the dandy dresses instead of living in earnest and rejects useful behaviour' (p.19). Because social satire is basic to all the plays of this type, the comedy of manners is a particularly subversive dramatic form. The men of fashion in the plays of the late seventeenth century defy the taboos of marriage: their life-style is aggressively promiscuous, hedonistic, yet ruthlessly cool. It is not surprising that in the eighteenth century the plays were rewritten (like Garrick's version of *The Country Wife* and Bickerstaff's *Plain Dealer*), adapted to suit the more urbane mood of the times; whilst in the nineteenth century they were effec- · tively ignored. In the dramas of Gilbert and Wilde conventional Victorian values are inverted and the comedy serves to reveal and attack social hypocrisy. Coward is very unconventional in the sexual morality he appears to advocate in his works: all his major plays in the comedy of manners style explore the impossibility of marriage. Osborne, the original 'angry young man', is no less a social critic because his style has matured, whilst Pinter has brought the threats so evident in his earlier drama from the realm of comedy of menace into that of comedy of manners. But it is Orton above all recent playwrights who has proved the most subversive and disturbing writer working in this field.

Two other features of this genre deserve mention. First, whilst ironic and witty social comedy has not been the prerogative of English playwrights — Molière and Beaumarchais in France and Albee in America have written extensively in this idiom — only in England has there been a continual development of comedy of manners as defined in this chapter and examined in the book as a whole. No doubt the peculiar richness of vocabulary and syntax possessed by the English language in part accounts for this, as well as the persistence of the subtle indestructible indications of our social class system. When, on the one hand, Pinter can exploit to such cunning effect the nuances and ambiguities of language, while, on the other hand, Ayckbourn can satirize the *mores* of specific clearly differentiated groups within the same (middle) class, we have proof of the abundant comic potential of this native tradition. These plays also require a distinctive style of acting: Edith Evans, John Gielgud, Vivien Merchant and Maggie Smith most notably have revealed a mastery of the comic technique which is basic to the understanding of this type of play in any period. Finally it is a significant fact that, despite the endurance of this branch of comedy, few plays have been written in this idiom by any one author. All the major comic dramatists of the late seventeenth century chose to abandon the theatre after writing a mere handful of plays; those dramatists, such as Coward and Maugham, who have been more prolific have again produced only a few works which may be strictly classified as comedies of manners. The very specific nature of the genre inevitably circumscribes its potential in the hands of any one author; but it is also perhaps significant that Wilde and Orton, who most fully exploited its savage satiric potential, and wrote as they lived — dangerously — should have led such short and tragic lives.

2

The seventeenth century

> I will believe, there are now in the world
> Good-natured friends, who are not prostitutes,
> And handsome women worthy to be friends:
> Yet, for my sake, let no one e'er confide
> In tears, or oaths, in love, or friend untried.
> (William Wycherley: *The Plain Dealer*, 1676)

The terms Restoration comedy and comedy of manners have become virtually synonymous; but in the twentieth century both require careful reconsideration. The comedy of manners is a dramatic genre which has continued in England to the present day; Restoration comedy has always been a curious misnomer: Charles II came to the throne in 1660, and to describe all the comedies of the next fifty years as 'Restoration' is meaningless. The term is perhaps meaningful when considering those plays written during Charles's reign, but to apply it to the dramas produced under James II, William and Mary and Queen Anne, whose political policies and life-style differed greatly, is absurd. Certainly the comedies written in these five decades have much in common which distinguished them from the Jacobean and early Caroline drama on the one hand and the plays of the later eighteenth century on the other. But it is equally instructive to observe that the plays of Farquhar, for example (the last two written in 1706 and 1707), have as much in common with *She Stoops to Conquer* as *The Country Wife* and indeed are much closer to Goldsmith's drama than to the plays of Sheridan, who is usually distinguished as the prime exponent of comedy of manners in the late eighteenth century. This chapter will examine the major comedies of the late seventeenth century, drawing attention to the recurrent themes which serve to classify them as a distinct dramatic genre, whilst also emphasizing the differences between the plays of dramatists working under different social and political conditions.

When the theatres reopened in England after the Restoration a distinct break in dramatic tradition and presentation had taken place. These theatres, at first only two — under the management of D'Avenant and Killigrew at Dorset Garden and Drury Lane respectively — were licensed by royal monopoly. They were much smaller than playhouses like the Globe and Swan, more on the model of the indoor Blackfriars, catering for an educated and wealthy aristocratic élite. The intimacy of the smaller indoor theatre with its proscenium and the beginnings of perspective scenery on grooved flats was a far cry from the Elizabethan outdoor public playhouse which had entertained an entire cross-section of the society of London. Shakespeare's theatre with its bare stage reflected the diversity and grandeur of Renaissance life; the Restoration playhouse represented only a few scenes: notably the coffee house, the drawing-room and the park, which defined and circumscribed the range of social behaviour examined by the dramatists. Restoration England was not an heroic age, in its accomplishments off-stage or on. In France Corneille's tragicomedies and Racine's tragedies were the perfect reflection of that tension between passion and intellect seen in the thought and action, both social and political, of Louis XIV's court and country.

The court of Charles II was a more cynical and licentious one, and on stage the dramatists, all of them in the truest sense dilettantes, because not fully committed professional men of the theatre, sought to reflect that freedom which was a deliberate counterpart to the Puritan repression of the interregnum. The presence of women for the first time on the English stage served to highlight the emphasis on marriage and sexual intrigue, with their corollaries, adultery and divorce: fresh themes for English comedy. Nor were they Molière's themes. In a stable country, during the Age of Reason, he attacked society's deviants and enemies. In England rebellion was the spirit of the age: Charles I lost his throne and head in 1649, James II his throne in 1688. Before the Puritan interregnum James I's Calvinist upbringing contrasted sharply with Charles I's Catholic sympathies which were inherited by his sons, Charles II and James II. The latter's open profession of Catholicism cost him his crown and he was replaced by William and Mary who handed on the Protestant succession to Queen Anne. Thus England knew no more stability than in the previous century, and saw as much bloody strife and more revolution. No wonder, then, that the immediate post-Restoration period saw drama, and notably comedy, that reflected the turbulence and dissatisfaction of the times. Comedy in the first two decades after the Restoration is notably satiric, savage, cruel, and, in so far as it deals seriously with the important issues of infidelity, marriage, divorce and another significant theme, money, essentially concerned with the incalcitrant realities of everyday life, fully reflecting the manners of a sexually and monetarily acquisitive society.

The plays of Wycherley are the most powerful dramatic expression of this post-Restoration spirit. Produced between 1671 and 1677, they are the most uncompromising comedies of the period, baldly stating several of the major themes which were to dominate the drama up to the beginning of the next century. His third play, *The Country Wife* (1674/5) has enjoyed most frequent revival — it was adapted by Garrick in the eighteenth century. Its title draws attention immediately to the contrast of rural and metropolitan values, so often a theme of comedy of manners. Margery, the country wife, has by the end of the play accepted the values of the metropolis: she has learnt how to lie, how to deceive her husband. Hoping to escape the consequences of an unhappy marriage to an old rake, now jealous to keep her to himself, she falls easy prey to Horner, the archetype of the Restoration rake or Don Juan figure. Knowing that decorum is all-important, Horner has penetrated the code of the times and exploits the hypocrisy of social manners to the utmost. In Act 1 he tells the Quack: 'your women of honour, as you call 'em, are only chary of their reputations, not their persons; and 'tis scandal they would avoid, not men' (I, i, ed. Jeffares, Vol. 1, p. 415) and proceeds to match this neat turn of phrase with an equally cool debauchery of all the available women, having circulated the false rumour that the incompetence of a French surgeon in curing venereal disease has made him sterile. The apparent frankness of this confession masks the unscrupulousness of his tactics: even as he disabuses the wives, he can abuse the husbands who flock to proffer their condolences.

As Margery's rustic ingenuousness gives way to determination she soon adapts to the ways of the world and to urban standards of behaviour. Wycherley gives such pointed physical emphasis to his satire that it is impossible to take sides: the playgoer is made forcefully aware of the cunning of the disloyal wives and friends whilst at the same time laughing at the vanity and folly of the dupes. Thus in V,i, when Margery encourages Pinchwife to lead her, masked and hooded, to her lover, we have no sympathy with the deceived husband who is quite prepared to prostitute, as he supposes, his innocent sister to the rake. This refusal to allow the audience a clear point of moral sympathy is basic to the genre and accounts for many critics' distaste of this comic mode. It occurs also in the sharply ironic scene (IV,i) in which Harcourt, disguised as a parson, masquerades as his own brother. The unscrupulousness of Harcourt, who here attempts to steal his own friend's mistress, is matched by the foolish vanity of Sparkish and the total inability of Alithea to cope with the situation, with the result that again the audience's sympathies are with the cleverest intriguer, who indeed wins the girl. Wycherley's plays are much concerned with the duplicity of bosom friends. In *The Gentleman Dancing-Master* (1672) Gerrard, in the act of stealing his friend's mistress, remarks to her: 'to make him hold the door while I steal his mistress is not unpleasant'; and to her objection: 'but it goes against my conscience to be accessory to so ill a thing' answers: 'Alas! poor miss, 'tis not against your conscience, but against your modesty, you think, to do it frankly' (IV,i, ed. Ward, pp. 208-9). This constant revelation of the gap between reality and appearance, between selfish motive and smooth professions of cordiality, is fundamental to the comedy of manners with its cynical view of conventional morality and lack of the romantic feeling central to other comic genres.

In its satiric as distinct from romantic emphasis the comedy of manners is in the tradition of Ben Jonson. Horner, at the centre of a complex plot with all the desirable women dancing attendance on him, is rather like Volpone or the alchemists, Subtle and Face. The comedies of the late seventeenth century, like those of Jonson earlier, are concerned with the unscrupulousness of the characters in pursuit of money and sex. But in Jonson money is a far more important concern: gulling and cozening are the activities of his wits, and Volpone is caught precisely because he falls a victim to his passion for Celia. Moreover, in Jonson's plays the cleverest do not always win; conventional morality, albeit subject to Jonson's ironic treatment, prevails, so that Mosca, Volpone, Subtle and Face are finally brought to justice. Enough traces of Jonsonian comedy remain, however, to make his influence clearly recognizable. From characters such as Dapperwit, Gripe and Addleplot in Wycherley's first play *Love in a Wood, or St James' Park* (1671), through to a play like Congreve's *The Old Bachelor* (1693), with its comic cuckold, Fondlewife, and its fools, Sir Jasper Wittol and Captain Bluffe, who are both tricked into marriage through the cunning of superior wits, the comedy of manners can be seen to be a development of the comedy of humours. Nor is it always easy to distinguish one dramatic genre precisely from the other. Vanbrugh's *The Confederacy* (1705), which dramatizes the parallel outwitting of two lustful old misers by their wives and a clever young lover, has affinities with both comedy of manners and Jacobean citizen comedy, though actually based on a French original, Dancourt's *Les Bourgeoises à la Mode*. Though Dryden in the *Essay of Dramatic Poesy* expressed unparalleled admiration for Jonson, the latter's influence is nowhere more clearly apparent than in Congreve's letter to John Dennis *Concerning Humour in Comedy*, where he defines humour as 'a singular and unavoidable manner of doing or saying anything, peculiar and natural to one man only: by which his speech and action are distinguished from those of other men' (*The Comedies of William Congreve*, ed. Marshall, p. 413). In the *Letter* he refers frequently to Jonson in support of his argument and uses *The Silent Woman* as an example to illustrate his basic theory — a significant one for the comedy of manners:

Humour is from Nature, *Habit* from Custom, and *Affection* from Industry.
Humour shows us as we *Are*.
Habit shows us as we appear under a forcible Impression.
Affectation shows what we would be, under a voluntary Disguise.
(*Ibid*, p. 410)

Epicoene, or The Silent Woman is an intriguing choice of play: whilst exploring the craft and subtlety of its intriguers and exposing affectation it is the ultimate comment on Renaissance sexuality and promiscuity. The silent woman turns out to be a boy, and the play, unlike those of the post-Restoration period, explores that complex bisexual world of Shakespeare's late comedies. The advent of the actress put an effective end to this Jacobean convention: after the Restoration comedy took an exclusively heterosexual theme.

Wycherley explores this sexual theme exhaustively. His

plays are concerned far more with sex than money. In *Love in a Wood* nearly all the major characters are in pursuit of more than one person. No one is actually married in this play, so that the savagery of the two mature comedies is lacking, but Ranger, the significantly-named hero, is the characteristic Restoration rake. Though he finally settles down with Lydia, the dénouement of the play is by no means conventionally romantic. Gripe, the 'covetous, lecherous old userer', outwits Dapperwit by marrying Lucy, thus avoiding payment of the sum exacted by her parents for an attempted rape, and hoping that he will beget children he excludes his daughter from her inheritance. Maria, the daughter, who has tricked both her father and future husband in contriving to marry when six months pregnant, is a typical Wycherley heroine. The romantic conventions of Shakespearian comedy are a far cry from the intrigues of the comedy of manners. Hippolyta in *The Gentleman Dancing-Master* is a sexually precocious heroine of fourteen. When caught with her lover she is not outwitted, but tells her father that Gerrard is her new dancing master: 'So much wit and innocency', he comments, 'were never together before.' By 'wit' he here means ingenuity and quick thinking in emergency. Another type of wit emerges in a later scene where the father insists on a continuation of the dancing lesson. Here the comments of Mrs Caution, 'an impertinent, precise old woman', though accurate, go unheeded, but they serve to underline the bawdy references:

> *Mrs Caution*: See, see, she squeezes his hand now: Oh, the debauched harlotry!
>
> *Don Diego*: So, so, mind her not; she moves forward pretty well; but you must move as well backward as forward, or you'll never do anything to purpose.
>
> *Mrs Caution*: Do you know what you say, brother, yourself, no? are you at your beastliness before your young daughter?
>
> (*The Gentleman Dancing Master*, II,i, ed. Ward, p. 186)

The bawdy, rather clumsy and repetitive in this early play, is refined in the celebrated 'china' scene of *The Country Wife*. Here not only is the allusiveness at once more pointed and subtle, but the dramatic circumstances enrich the humour by giving an added sharpness to the irony. Both Mrs Squeamish and Lady Fidget believe each alone shares Horner's secret, but as the scene develops the increasing twists in the bawdy *double entendre* express a growing anxiety and sexual jealousy on the part of two women, all the more intense because of the strained euphemisms they employ. This is Wycherley at his best, exactly suiting the witty style to his predominantly sexual theme. It contrasts pointedly with the refinement of dialogue in Congreve and the urbanity of style which distinguishes the plays of Farquhar, but all three dramatists in different ways employ wit to define character and present the complex ironies of a dramatic situation:

Lady Fidget: And I have been toiling and moiling, for the prettiest piece of china, my dear.
Horner: Nay, she has been too hard for me, do what I could.
Mrs Squeamish: Oh Lord, I'll have some china too, good Mr Horner, don't think to give other people china, and me none, come in with me too.
Horner: Upon my honour, I have none left now.
Mrs Squeamish: Nay, nay, I have known you deny your china before now, but you shan't put me off so. Come —
Horner: This lady had the last there.
Lady Fidget: Yes indeed, Madam, to my certain knowledge he has no more left.
Mrs Squeamish: O, but it may be he may have some you could not find.
(*The Country Wife,* IV,iii, Jeffares Vol. 1, p. 478)

Wycherley sees women as unscrupulous predators; men are ultimately their pawns in the love game. This is true even of Horner; perhaps most of all in his case if we are to take the view expressed in Warren Beatty's film *Shampoo*, a clever modern version of *The Country Wife*, in which the central character uses the rumours of alleged homosexuality as a cover for his various amours. Finally he sees the worthlessness of his situation, a position Horner himself does not reach, though the existential quality of the film finds its parallel in the obsessive harping on images of disease — particularly venereal disease — in the play, an effective reminder of the occupational hazard Horner runs, a danger all too familiar to the Restoration rake.

Wycherley's last play *The Plain Dealer* (1676/7), an adaptation of Molière's *Le Misanthrope*, is his most uncompromising work. In his reworking of ideas from several of Molière's plays, most notably *L'Ecole des Femmes* and *L'Ecole des Maris* (for *The Country Wife*) Wycherley brought certain aspects of contemporary French comedy — notably its refinement of style and treatment of social manners — to the English stage. But his handling of the material from Molière shows how Wycherley's plays, and indeed the whole genre of comedy of manners in England differed radically from French concepts of drama and satire. Molière's plays cannot be neatly categorized in any one specific dramatic genre: whilst *Le Misanthrope* could be termed a comedy of manners, such works as *Le Malade Imaginaire* and *L'Avare* are closer to farce and draw on the conventions of the *commedia dell' arte*, whilst mature dramas such as *Dom Juan* and *Tartuffe* powerfully and disturbingly mingle different theatrical styles. Wycherley's adaption of *Le Misanthrope* deepens and extends the satire of Molière's play, introducing new themes vital to the English comedy of manners, as he makes clearer the vices of the age he is so determined to scourge. Alceste, Molière's misanthrope, is an outsider, an excessive critic who will not listen to his friend, the *raisonneur* and exponent of the virtue of the 'honnête homme', Philinte. His mistress, Célimene, is not vicious: she is beautiful, witty and charming, a flirt, but finally, in her refusal to accompany Alceste to the country, a reasonable repudiator of his standards. Society around Alceste is bitchy and opportunist, but there are enough selfless and sensible figures to counteract this. Molière (to quote Jonson) 'sports with human follies, not with crimes': in a balanced age of reason he criticizes those who offend a social norm, and Alceste is the worst offender. This is not the picture in Wycherley's play; the society he presents is so unscrupulous in its attitude to love, marriage and money that Manly, the plain dealer of the title, though a sailor and thus a more obvious social outsider than Alceste, is right to despise and mistrust the world.

Manly's bosom and only friend, Vernish, is so only in appearance. He is actually secretly married to Manly's mistress, Olivia, and the pair of them are out to make all the money they can from Manly. They make a very sinister impression on Vernish's first appearance:

> *Olivia*: Manly is returned.
>
> *Vernish*: Manly returned! Fortune forbid! . . . did you own our marriage to him?
>
> *Olivia*: I told him I was married, to put an end to his love, and my trouble; but to whom, is yet a secret kept from him, and all the world: and I have used him so scurvily, his great spirit will ne'er return, to reason it farther with me; I have sent him to sea again, I warrant.
>
> *Vernish*: Twas bravely done . . . Be you sure only to keep a while our great secret, till he be gone: in the meantime, I'll lead the easy honest fool by the nose, as I used to do; and, whilst he stays, rail with him at thee; and, when he's gone, laugh with thee at him. But have you his cabinet of jewels safe? Part not with a seed pearl to him, to keep him from starving.
>
> *Olivia*: Nor from hanging.
>
> (*The Plain Dealer*, IV,ii, ed. Jeffares, Vol. 2, p. 189)

The unscrupulousness of the characters is extreme here. We have not yet the refinement of intrigue which distinguishes the subtlest characters in Congreve's plays, but no one went further than Wycherley in satirizing the rapaciousness of the times. Olivia in the above scene is surprised by her husband's return: she is waiting for the arrival of a new lover, Manly's servant, and having 'thrust out' her husband she says, 'So, I have at once brought about those two grateful businesses, which all prudent women do together, secured money and pleasure' (*ibid*, IV,ii, p. 190). However, the servant is in fact a woman, Fidelia, in disguise; she has become entangled in this situation through love of Manly. Wycherley's employment of the disguise convention differs from the romantic dramas of Shakespeare or Beaumont and Fletcher in pointing up the viciousness of Olivia and the folly of both Fidelia and Manly, as in the sequel to the scene described above, when Fidelia arrives with Manly 'treading softly and staying behind at some distance', where again Wycherley exploits the physical ironies of the situation to full satiric effect.

Olivia is seen at her worst in a scene Wycherley added to the play in a later revision, and which takes its cue from Scene vi of Molière's *La Critique de L'Ecole des Femmes*. Here Wycherley employs a discussion of *The Country Wife* to present the hypocrisy and prudery of Olivia and thereby to throw into ironic relief the arguments concerning moral impropriety in his plays, and indeed those of the genre as a whole.

> *Olivia*: Then you would have a woman of honour with passive looks, ears and tongue, undergo all the hideous obscenity she hears at nasty plays?
> *Eliza*: Truly, I think a woman betrays her want of modesty, by showing it publicly in a playhouse, as much as a man does his want of courage by a quarrel there: for the truly modest and stout say least, and are least exceptious, especially in public.
> *Olivia*: O hideous! cousin, this cannot be your opinion, but you are one of those that have the confidence to pardon

the filthy play.

Eliza: Why, what is there of ill in't, say you?

Olivia: O fie, fie, fie, would you put me to the blush anew? Call all the blood into my face again? But, to satisfy you then, first, the clandestine obscenity in the very name of Horner.

Eliza: Truly, 'tis so hidden, I cannot find it out, I confess.

Olivia: O horrid! Does it not give you the rank conception, or image of a goat, a town-bull, or a satyr?

(*Ibid*, II,i, p. 136)

Wycherley's satire here anticipates the Jeremy Collier stage controversy which broke out two decades later and continued well into the eighteenth century. The significance of Collier's pamphlet *A Short View of the Immorality and Profaneness of the English Stage*, published in 1698, is evident in the fact that many leading writers, notably Vanbrugh and Congreve, felt the need to reply to his attack on 'their smuttiness of expression, their swearing, profaneness and lewd application of scripture, their abuse of the clergy, their making their top characters libertines and giving them success in their debauchery' (*A Short View*, p.2). The twentieth-century response to the criticisms of the 'frenzied divine' (as Bonamy Dobrée calls him) has generally been one of amused contempt, but it is a mark of the change which had come about in the religious and moral climate of the country by the end of the seventeenth century that he should have been taken so seriously, and that Dr Johnson could say: 'at last comedy grew more modest and Collier lived to see the reward of his labours'.

Etherege, Wycherley's close contemporary, paints a similar picture of the ruthlessness of society at the beginning of this period, though with less savagery and bitterness. In his final and most celebrated play, *The Man of Mode* (1676), Mrs Loveit reaches the conclusion: 'There's nothing but falsehood and impertinence in this world. All men are villains or fools'

(*The Man of Mode*, V,ii, ed. Jeffares, Vol. 1, p. 618), and she has said earlier: 'There is no truth in friendship neither. Women, as well as men, are all false, or all are so to me at least' (*ibid*, V,i, p. 600). The final phrase is significant: she is speaking as a loser, and Etherege wastes little sympathy on her; but this does not detract from the truth of her remarks. Mrs Loveit tries throughout the play to win back Dorimant who has tired of her; he has designs on her close friend Belinda as well as a newcomer to the city, the wealthy young heiress, Harriet. By the end of the play he has achieved all he wanted: he has made love to Belinda, rid himself of Mrs Loveit, and Harriet is prepared to marry him. Here we have an early glimpse of the higher stakes for which the characters are playing, though Dorimant is a novice beside Fainall and Mirabel. He is essentially interested in sex, and it is some consolation for Mrs Loveit to learn that he needs Harriet as 'a wife to repair the ruins of my estate that needs it'. Moreover the hollowness of his victory, in contrast to that of Mirabel or Archer, is seen in the way Harriet paints an uninspired picture of what life with her will be like. To her mother's offer: 'you will be welcome', she adds:

> To a great rambling lone house, that looks as it were not inhabited, the family's so small; there you'll find my mother, an old lame aunt, and myself, Sir, perched upon chairs at a distance in a large parlour; sitting moping like three or four melancholy birds in a spacious volary. Does not this stagger your resolution? (*Ibid*, V,ii, p. 619).

Having had a glimpse of life in the metropolis, Harriet is unwilling to go back to the country. That she has more wit and sensitivity than Margery Pinchwife only exacerbates her situation, which was clear enough in her conversation with Young Bellair earlier in the play:

> *Young Bellair*: What a dreadful thing 'twould be to be hurried back to Hampshire!
> *Harriet*: Ah, — name it not!   (*Ibid*, III,i, p. 559)

When at the end of the play (V,ii) Dorimant makes light of these difficulties and says: 'The first time I saw you, you left me with the pangs of love upon me, and this day my soul has quite given up her liberty', she retorts: 'This is more dismal than the country.'

Whether she is more distressed by his insincerity or the warmth of his changed manner is not clear, but this twist at the end points up the unromantic aspect of the dénouement. The play is much concerned with tone, style and the dangers of sincerity. Mrs Loveit comes nearest to regaining her hold on Dorimant when she pretends to love Sir Fopling Flutter; though Dorimant does not believe her, he is horrified to find that the mere suspicion arouses his jealousy and thus his renewed interest in her. The plays of the period are rich in such acute observations of psychological and sexual truths, often startling in their apparent modernity; thus in *The Country Wife* (III,ii) Sparkish makes the Pinteresque observation: 'I love to have rivals in a wife, they make her seem to a man still but as a kept mistress', and in *The Old Bachelor* Lucy tells her mistress, Sylvia, that the way to win back Vainlove is to make him believe not that Araminta is in love with someone else, but that she returns his love. In the long scene between Mrs Loveit and Dorimant (V,i) Mrs Loveit is in control so long as she can counter Dorimant's objections to Sir Fopling with the controlled power of her perfectly phrased epigrams. The savagery of his jealousy, finding its expression in sharp, cutting images, is contrasted with the calculated tone of her rejoinders:

Mrs Loveit: The man who loves above his quality, does not suffer more from the insolent impertinence of his mistress, than the woman who loves above her understanding does from the arrogant presumptions of her friend.
Dorimant: You mistake the use of fools, they are designed for properties and not for friends, you have an indifferent stock of reputation left yet. Lose it all like a frank games-

ter on the square, 'twill then be time enough to turn rook,
and cheat it up again on a good substantial bubble.

Mrs Loveit: The old man and the ill-favoured are only fit for
properties indeed, but young and handsome fools have
met with kinder fortunes.

(*Ibid*, V,i, p. 604).

It is clear who has the upper hand at this point; the style here
tells us everything: emotional aggression is translated into the
cut and thrust of images and phrases. This is the essence of comedy of manners: what T.S. Eliot describes as the 'dissociation
of sensibility' has not yet taken place: mind and emotion are
fused in the invention and sustaining of witty dialogue. Etherege, however, forces us to watch a break occur disturbingly at
the end of the scene. Firmly defeated by Mrs Loveit's control
of language and the situation, Dorimant is about to leave,
whereupon Mrs Loveit fatally drops the mask of civilized argument. 'I hate that nauseous fool, you know I do', she admits,
thus by one frank sentence undermining all the power she had
established over Dorimant. This confession is a form of extravagance, the trait she elsewhere manifests in her more open pursuit of Dorimant and notably in the scene (II,ii) where she
resorts to the impotent rage of uttering the oath 'Hell and
furies', then tears her fan in pieces and finally bursts into tears.
In this respect Sir Fopling is her equal: his extravagance is of
dress and affected speech. Dorimant, the true beau, sees the
importance of appearance — the play opens with a long scene
in his dressing room as he is absorbed in his levée — but this is
for him something more: a mask and a means to an end. Sir
Fopling, however, is all show; there is nothing beneath the surface. Like Mrs Loveit, he will be outmanoeuvred, though he
does pose a threat, not only in his wooing of Mrs Loveit, but
also in his way of life, as Emilia is quick to point out: 'However
you despise him gentlemen, I'll lay my life he passes for a wit
with many.' Dorimant draws our attention in his reply to the

importance of critical discernment, the corollary of good taste: 'That may very well be, nature has her cheats, stums a brain, and puts sophisticate dullness often on the tasteless multitude for true wit and good humour' (*ibid*, III,ii, pp. 568-9). This, for a civilized courtier and dandy like Etherege, was the final word. It was Congreve at the end of the century who, in his presentation of men like Tattle, Witwoud and Petulant, was to explore the satiric potential of this 'sophisticate dullness'.

It is revealing to contrast the plays of Wycherley and Etherege, written at the beginning of the post-Restoration period, with those of Farquhar written thirty years later at the beginning of the eighteenth century. In the Prologue to his last play, *The Beaux' Stratagem* (1707) Farquhar sums up the temper of this very different era:

> When strife disturbs or sloth corrupts an age,
> Keen satire is the business of the stage.
> When the Plain-Dealer writ he lashed those crimes
> Which then infested most — the modish times:
> But now, when faction sleeps, and sloth is fled,
> And all our youth in active fields are bred . . .
> There scarce is room for satire.
> (*The Beaux' Stratagem,* Jeffares, Vol. 4, p. 411)

This was written in 1707 during the reign of Queen Anne, whilst the War of the Spanish Succession was being fought. Civil war had given place to victorious conquest abroad; England had a right to feel secure. This was a new century, a more rational age, benefiting from the writing of men like Locke and the discoveries of scientists like Newton. The task of the critic and dramatic artist was no longer to 'lash crimes' but to ridicule 'follies', as Farquhar goes on to say:

> Simpling our author goes from field to field,
> And culls such fools, as may diversion yield.
> (*Ibid*, p. 411)

The satire of this age is milder, more urbane, and yet in

several important respects the dramas are more serious. The Restoration rake avoided the traps of matrimony through promiscuity and adultery; to an essentially pro-Catholic age this was the only way out. But under the Protestant monarchs, William and Mary and Queen Anne, another solution was considered: divorce. The fates to which Margery Pinchwife and Mrs Sullen can respectively look forward are a nice indication of the morals of the different periods, though Mrs Sullen's position is more complex than may at first appear. At the end of *The Beaux Stratagem* she is free of her husband and can look forward to a happier life with Archer, who says:

> Consent, if mutual, saves the lawyer's fee,
> Consent is law enough to set you free.
> (*Ibid*, V,iv, p. 496)

That this is manifestly untrue — by law she was as securely trapped as Margery — does not undermine Farquhar's ending; the worlds of the theatre and of real life are different and his more romantic ending is in spirit with the development of the action throughout. It is more reasonable to object that the seriousness with which he advocates the case for divorce is at variance with the play's dénouement which, in its avoidance of the harsh facts of reality, anticipates the sentimentality of later eighteenth-century comedies. This is most pronounced in III,iii where, drawing very directly on Milton's Book II of *Doctrine and Discipline of Divorce* (published 1643), he makes Mrs Sullen argue persuasively for a more humane approach:

> *Mrs Sullen*: Law! What law can search into the remote abyss of nature, what evidence can prove the unaccountable disaffections of wedlock — can a jury sum up the endless aversions that are rooted in our souls, or can a bench give judgement upon antipathies.
>
> *Dorinda*: They never pretended sister, they never meddle but in case of uncleanness.
>
> *Mrs Sullen*: Uncleanness! O sister, casual violation is a tran-

sient injury, and may possibly be repaired, but can radical hatreds be ever reconciled — No, no, sister, nature is the first lawgiver, and when she has set tempers opposite, not all the golden links of wedlock, nor iron manacles of law can keep 'um fast.

> (*Ibid*, III,iii, pp. 456-7)

This translates the forcefulness of Milton into a more measured, but no less persuasive prose which leads smoothly into the heroic couplets which close the act as Mrs Sullen advances to address the audience with added force:

> Wedlock we own ordained by heaven's decree,
> But such as heaven ordained it first to be,
> Concurring tempers in the man and wife
> As mutual helps to draw the load of life . . .
> Must man, the chiefest work of art divine,
> Be doomed in endless discord to repine,
> No, we should injure heaven by that surmise
> Omnipotence is just, were man but wise.
> (*Ibid*, p. 457).

No passage more clearly illustrates the affinity of Farquhar's style with the urbanity of Pope. The anticipation here of 'An Essay on Man' throws into relief the contrast with the earlier dramatists and notably with Wycherley, whose restless energy and savagery of expression are in the satiric vein of Dryden.

Archer's wooing of Mrs Sullen in IV,i further illustrates the warmth and ease which characterizes the witty dialogue in this play. By contrast with the forceful bawdy of the 'china' episode in *The Country Wife* or the sharply polished exchanges of Mirabel and Millament in their 'contract' scene, a subtlety of sexual innuendo (mixed with discreet flattery) pervades Archer's seduction of Mrs Sullen. Before she knows what is happening Archer has lured her into the bedroom. Her modesty forces her to run out, though the intervention at this point of Scrub, Sullen's servant, would have guaranteed her honour's safety. Such is the nature of Farquhar's plot that no one is ever in serious danger. Though Mrs Sullen admits to Dorinda a little later: 'I can't swear I could resist the temptation, — though I can safely promise to avoid it; and that's as much as the best of us can do' (IV,i) — a very rational approach to the situation and a far cry from the attitudes of Mrs Loveit or Lady Fidget — there is no real threat to her safety. When Archer gains entrance to her bedroom later she is a match for him. Her frequent confessions of weakness to the audience are belied by such comments as 'Rise, thou prostrate engineer, not all thy undermining skill shall reach my heart', a repulse worthy of Lady Bracknell (V,ii); and just as he appears to be gaining the upper hand Scrub rushes in again, this time with news of housebreakers.

The fates of the characters are determined not only by their own actions, but by external forces which play havoc with their neat plans. In this respect Farquhar's drama differs radically from that of Wycherley, Etherege and Congreve, in whose plays the characters are entirely responsible for the outcome of their own actions and where it is the cleverest player who wins the game and takes all. Moreover in Farquhar the better natures of the characters are apt to take over just when victory seems in view. Thus Archer relinquishes his seduction of Mrs Sullen to defend her life, and Aimwell confesses to Dorinda the stratagem the two friends have employed to give a false impression of their incomes. Both are rewarded, Aimwell by learning that he has miraculously inherited the title of Lord Viscount through the timely death of his brother, and Archer by profiting from Captain Gibbet's rifling of Sullen's escritoire. Both the initial stratagem of the two beaux and their ruse to gain entrance to Sullen's house are more broadly and overtly comic than any such tricks in earlier comedies of manners, and it is a measure of the more genial tone of this play that Gibbet should be a sentimental highwayman, Boniface a sanguine rogue and Cherry a shrewd country girl. This play is set in Lichfield, and *The Recruiting Officer* in Shrewsbury: by this date the accepted superiority of metropolitan over provincial manners has given way to a tempering of the ruthlessness of city affairs by a natural warmth and openness. Thus Archer criticizes Aimwell: 'you can't counterfeit the passion without feeling it', but he nevertheless respects and remains true to his friend, a very different attitude from that assumed by the characters in Wycherley, Etherege or Congreve.

Farquhar's other mature play, *The Recruiting Officer* (1706), is less concerned with sex and money. The wit in this play resides in the complex machinations whereby Sylvia obeys the letter of her promise to her father, but disobeys him in essence by obliging him in court to hand her over to Plume. Money in this play, far from being an incentive to the lovers, is a hindrance: both Worthy and Plume consider Mellinda and Sylvia temporarily lost when each woman inherits a fortune. It is characteristic of Farquhar's comedy that fortunes are so easily won: in Congreve the characters have to work for them. The military theme of the play initially gives added depth and toughness to the comedy of manners, but this develops later into a more farcical plot and romantic dénouement. William Gaskill's direction of these two plays at the National Theatre (in 1963 and 1970), however, marked an important stage in the re-establishment of the comedy of manners, since he chose to direct them in an almost Brechtian, realistic style. He laid emphasis on motivation and human relationships, not on external mannerisms or superficiality of style which had characterized the revivals of Congreve and Farquhar by Nigel Playfair and John Gielgud earlier in the century. Of the production of *The Recruiting Officer* Tynan said: 'A Restoration masterpiece has been reclaimed, stripped of the veneer of camp that custom prescribes for such plays and saved for the second half of the twentieth century' (Introduction to his edition of the National Theatre production (London, 1965), p. 16). Moreover Réné Allio's simple, deliberately two-dimensional sets, changed in full view of the audience, found, in the case of both

productions, a subtle equivalent for the Restoration stage
which, in its contrast of acting area and pictorial scene, mir-
rored what Clifford Leech has called 'the tension between the
individual figures and the society which imposes conventions,
expectations, circumspection' (*Restoration Drama, Modern
Essays in Criticism*, ed. Loftis, p. 134).

Farquhar's plays have many affinities with those of Van-
burgh. Like Lady Brute, the provoked wife of Vanbrugh's
play, Mrs Sullen has grounds for infidelity. In the witty seduction scene of *The Provoked Wife* (1697) Constant remarks:
'But since you are already disposed of beyond redemption, to
one who does not know the value of the jewel you have put into
his hands, I hope you would not think him greatly wronged,
though it should sometimes be looked on by a friend who
knows how to esteem it as he ought' (*The Provoked Wife*, III,i,
ed. Jeffares, Vol. 3, p. 604). This extends the clever play on language which earlier in the scene centred on monetary transactions whilst forwarding a seduction. Vanbrugh gives an added
seriousness by intertwining the two central themes of the genre
in a conversation which anticipates Archer's wooing of Mrs
Sullen:

> *Constant*: I hope you'll have so favourable an opinion of my
>   understanding too, to believe the thing called virtue has
>   worth enough with me, to pass for an eternal obligation
>   where'er 'tis sacrificed.
> *Lady Brute*: It is, I think, so great a one, as nothing can
>   repay.
> *Constant*: Yes; the making the man you love your everlast-
>   ing debtor.
> *Lady Brute*: When debtors once have borrowed all we have
>   to lend, they are very apt to grow very shy of their credi-
>   tors' company.
> *Constant*: That, Madam, is only when they are forced to bor-
>   row of usurers, and not of a generous friend.
>   (*Ibid*, III,i, p. 603)

Through the clever extension of this image the audience is made as aware as the characters of the seriousness of the situation. Lady Brute is contemplating adultery and in this play there is no discussion of divorce. As in Farquhar's play, however, the consummation of the act is foiled, here by the machinations of Lady Fanciful, a more broadly comic and less dangerous intriguer than Marwood in *The Way of the World*, with whom she has a superficial affinity. The central issue of adultery is indeed never carried to a proper conclusion in this play, because the unmasking of Lady Fanciful and the marriage of Heartfree and Belinda distract attention from the more serious subject of the Brutes.

A similar avoidance of adultery on the part of the wronged wife occurs in *The Relapse* (1697), a drama which throws light on the *mores* of the late seventeenth century and notably on the different codes which distinguished the conduct of men from that of women. Amanda, married to Loveless, is tempted to have an affair with Worthy because of her husband's relapse into adultery. Unknown to her, his mistress is in fact her friend, Berinthia, who has encouraged Loveless's advances in order that Worthy, her ex-lover, may enjoy Amanda. The Loveless —Berinthia relationship is concluded with Loveless carrying Berinthia into the bedroom as she says, 'very softly', 'Help, help, I'm ravish'd, ruin'd, undone. O Lord I shall never be able to bear it' (*The Relapse*, IV,iii, ed. Jeffares, Vol. 3, p. 512). Manners dictate that she make a token resistance, no more; her complicity is taken for granted. A wife's infidelity is another matter, however, and Vanbrugh causes Amanda to refuse her lover at the last moment, but with such grace that he exclaims:

'What but now was the wild flame of love,
  Or (to dissect that specious term)
  The vile, the gross desires of flesh and blood,
  Is in a moment turned to adoration'. (*Ibid*, V,iv, p. 542)

There is a more pointed contrast between the Loveless—

Amanda—Berinthia—Worthy scheme and the completely separate plot which concerns the rivalry between Young Fashion and Lord Foppington for the hand of Hoyden. Here the monetary theme is in evidence — both are pursuing this awkward country girl solely for her inheritance. But Vanbrugh does not treat this subject with the seriousness accorded the sexual conspiracy. Instead we are presented with a farcical comedy of situation resolved by a convenient twist of fortune whereby Young Fashion — a role played by an actress, Mrs Kent, *en travestie* in the first production — gains the money from Fatgoose living.

The complete separation of the two plots in this play, written in 1696, further highlights the distinctive qualities of comedy of manners as distinct from romantic or sentimental comedy. In the city, which breeds the affected conduct of Lord Foppington and entangles Loveless as soon as he leaves his sheltered pastoral retreat, sophisticated intrigue characterizes the relationships of the lovers, and it is their plotting which determines the course of the action. As in Elizabethan romantic comedy, the story which centres on Hoyden reveals by contrast that mistaken identity and untimely arrivals place the outcome of events beyond the control of the characters and in the hands of a benevolent fate.

It is in the plays of Congreve that we find the ultimate refinement of those themes we have so far observed as characteristic features of the comedy of manners. His first play, *The Old Bachelor* (1693), reveals a mixture of styles, but it points forward to the uncompromising presentation of human conduct in *The Way of the World* (1700). This first play, like his most romantic and popular comedy *Love for Love* (1695), ends with a dance which, as in Shakespearian comedy, celebrates the forthcoming marriages. But the action which has preceded this conventional dénouement observes more Restoration standards of behaviour. Bellmour, who finally marries Belinda, has earlier in the play been disturbed in his seduction of Laetitia by her husband, the banker, Fondlewife. Laetitia was pursued initially by Bellmour's friend, Vainlove, who hands her over once he becomes more interested in Araminta. Bellmour's comment on this situation reveals (with an appropriately neat turn of phrase) the coolness of the amoral debauchee:

> *Bellmour*: Why, what a cormorant in love am I! who, not contented with the slavery of honourable love in one place, and the pleasure of enjoying some half a score mistresses of my own acquiring, must yet take Vainlove's business upon my hands, because it lay too heavy on his: so am not only forced to lie with other men's wives for 'em, but must also undertake the harder task of obliging their mistresses.
>
> (*The Old Bachelor*, I,i, ed. Marshall, pp. 46-7)

Bellmour's interest in Belinda, however, stems from quite a different motive: money; and his remark to Vainlove later in the scene: 'There's twelve thousand pounds, Tom — 'Tis true she is excessively foppish and affected; but in my conscience I believe the baggage loves me', reveals the arrogant assurance of the womanizer. He assures Belinda later: 'courtship to marriage, is but the music in the playhouse till the curtain's drawn; but that once up, then opens the scene of pleasure'; but Belinda's response is more in tune with the play's overall tone and the cynical note of its dénouement: 'Oh, foh! no; rather courtship to marriage, is as a very witty prologue to a very dull play' (*ibid*, V,iv. p. 100).

The Way of the World, like the most complex and richest comedies of manners from Wycherley through to Pinter, is more concerned with the 'play' than the 'prologue', and *The Old Bachelor* further anticipates this mature comedy in its emphasis on the importance of relations established prior to the play's action as well as in its presentation of the higher stakes, money and matrimony, for which the characters are playing. *The Double Dealer* (1694) has further affinities with *The Way of the World* in its contrast between intriguers cunningly employing wit to outmanoeuvre their rivals and affected wits who waste their ingenuity on mere words. Maskwell is an ancestor of Fainall (the parts were both played by Betterton, just as the heroines Araminta, Cynthia, Angelica and Millamant were created by Mrs Bracegirdle whilst the roles of the more cunning and licentious women, Laetitia, Lady Touchwood, Mrs Frail and Marwood were written for Mrs Barry); the *dramatis personae* describes him as 'a villain; pretended friend to Mellefont, gallant to Lady Touchwood, and in love with Cynthia' — which is a fair indication of Congreve's debt to Wycherley in combining and further extending the complexity of roles a character can assume. The final defeat of Maskwell, by an inferior in intelligence, his dupe Mellefont, contrasts with the astringent tone Congreve employs in *The Way of the World*. Maskwell's perceptive insight into human nature sets him above the other characters: in soliloquy he reflects (of Lady Touchwood):

> Pox! I have lost all appetite to her; yet she's a fine woman, and I loved her once. But I don't know, since I have been in great measure kept by her, the case is altered; what was my pleasure is become my duty: and I have as little stomach to her now as if I were her husband . . . Pox on't! That a man can't drink without quenching his thirst.
>
> (*The Double Dealer*, III,i, ed. Marshall, p. 157)

The cynicism here has an undeniable ring of truth and it is a mark of sentimentality and dishonesty, therefore, that Maskwell is finally outwitted. Cynthia's love for Mellefont is also unrealistic in her disregard for money, though Congreve reveals that his heroine demands wit as well as passion in her lover, when she says: "tis but reasonable that since I consent to like a man without the vile consideration of money, he should give me a very evident demonstration of his wit; therefore let me see you undermine my Lady Touchwood, as you boasted. . .' (*ibid*, IV,i, p. 170).

Such a challenge has a parallel in Angelica's testing of Valentine in *Love for Love*, a play which in its presentation of the way Mrs Frail and Tattle are trapped into marriage and in its characterization of Foresight harks back to Jonson again, whilst anticipating the dramas of the eighteenth century in the broader comedy arising both from Valentine's disguise of madness to cheat his surly father and the uncouth behaviour of Ben and Prue. It is in the scene between Prue and Tattle that Congreve plays his most subtly amusing variation on the theme of the town versus the country, where the confrontation of the affected wit and the ingenuous young girl throws metropolitan manners into sharply ironic relief:

> *Prue*: Well; and how will you make love to me — Come, I long to have you begin; — Must I make love too? You must tell me how.
> *Tattle*: You must let me speak Miss, you must not speak first; I must ask you questions, and you must answer.
> *Prue*: What, is it like the catechism? — Come then ask me.
> *Tattle*: D'ye think you can love me?
> *Prue*: Yes.
> *Tattle*: Pooh, pox, you must not say yes already; I shan't care a farthing for you then in a twinkling.
> *Prue*: What must I say then?
> *Tattle*: Why you must say no, or you believe not, or you can't tell.
> *Prue*: Why, must I tell a lie then?
> *Tattle*: Yes, if you would be well bred.
>   (*Love for Love*, II,i, ed. Jeffares, Vol. 3, p. 271)

The final exchange in the above conversation points up an attitude fundamental to comedy of manners, acting also as a relevant comment on the conduct of the characters in this play's very different sequel, *The Way of the World*. From the start it is clear that every person in this play is involved in a ruthless battle of wits in which the stakes are very high. Congreve emphasizes this later by furnishing us with specific details, not-

ably in V,vi, where Fainall appears to have the upper hand
entirely: he has control of Lady Wishfort's estate, the whole of
his wife's fortune and Millamant's £6,000 share. His conduct
is, as Lady Wishfort says, 'most inhumanely savage', but he is
finally outwitted by Mirabell, his true match (as Mellefont is
not Maskwell's), who gains wife, compliant mistress and fortune because he has ensured the servants' allegiance — by see-
ing that Foible marries Waitwell — and has persuaded
Arabella to sign a deed of conveyance of her whole estate to
him before marrying Fainall. At that time she was Mirabell's
mistress: earlier in the play he points out unemotionally why he
did not marry her:

> *Mirabell*: Why do we daily commit disagreeable and danger-
> ous actions? To save that idol reputation. If the familiari-
> ties of our loves had produced that consequence, of
> which you were apprehensive, where could you have
> fixed a father's name with credit, but on a husband? I
> knew Fainall to be a man lavish of his morals, an inter-
> ested and professing friend, a false and a designing lover;
> yet one whose wit and outward fair behaviour have
> gained a reputation with the Town, enough to make that
> woman stand excused, who has suffered herself to be
> won by his addresses. A better man ought not to have
> been sacrificed to the occasion; a worse had not answered
> the purpose.
>
> (*The Way of the World*, II,i, ed. Jeffares, Vol. 4,
> p. 135)

The development of the plot depends throughout on the complexity of relationships which have a history stretching back
long prior to the play's action. Fainall's quarrel with Marwood
in Act II illustrates how the delicate balance of roles — husband, lover, friend, mistress, wife — is easily disturbed:

> *Fainall*: 'Twas for my ease to oversee and wilfully neglect
> the gross advances made him by my wife; that, by permit-

ting her to be engaged, I might continue unsuspected in my pleasures; and take you oftener to my arms in full security. But could you think because the nodding husband would not wake, that e'er the watchful lover slept.

(*Ibid*, II,i, p. 132)

He suspects Marwood here because she has informed Lady Wishfort of Mirabell's true motive in pretending love to her:

Fainall: Your fame I have preserved. Your fortune has been bestowed as the prodigality of your love would have it, in pleasures which we both have shared. Yet had not you been false, I had e'er this repaid it — Tis true — Had you permitted Mirabell with Millamant to have stolen their marriage, my lady had been incensed beyond all measure of reconcilement: Millamant had forfeited the moeity of her fortune; which would then have descended to my wife, — And wherefore did I marry, but to make lawful prize of a rich widow's wealth, and squander it on love and you.

(*Ibid*, p. 134)

His logic is inexorable; from the start sexual and monetary motives are seen to be closely interrelated and, moreover, to determine entirely the development of the action.

The resolution of the plot is brought about according to very precise rules defined by documents and contracts. Fittingly, the proposal scene between Mirabell and Millamant has strong legal overtones as the two employ their wit to drive the best bargain. At the end of her list of requirements Millamant states: 'These articles subscribed, if I continue to endure you a little longer, I may by degrees dwindle into a wife', whilst Mirabell, after laying down his conditions, concludes: 'These provisos admitted, in other things I may prove a tractable and complying husband' (*ibid*, IV,i, pp. 169 and 171). The coolness of their tone should not deceive us into believing that their relationship is as empty as that of Arabella and Fainall: rather the intensity of the witty conflict is indicative of the depth of their emotional commitment and the fact that they are perfectly matched. This conversation, however, is preceded by a scene between Millamant and her provincial suitor, Sir Wilfull Witwoud, which, like the scene between Tattle and Prue, throws the question of style into a more ironic perspective. By contrast with Sir Wilfull's rough honesty Millamant's wit here seems affected and arrogant. She finds his conversation 'rustic, ruder than gothic' and adds 'I nauseate walking; 'tis a country diversion, I loathe the country and everything that relates to it'. This reveals the complete dismissal of rural values by a skilful exponent of the manners of the town. But Mirabell and Millamant play by the rules these manners dictate, and it is the fine balance they maintain between emotion and reason which ensures their victory over the unfeeling Fainall, the jealous Marwood and the foolish Lady Wishfort whose longing for a 'pastoral solitude' is as false and empty as the affected manners of Witwoud and Petulant.

The proviso scene pre-eminently illustrates the interdependence of theatrical dialogue and the language of the civilized society of the day. Congreve dedicated the play to Ralph, Earl of Montague and admitted: 'If it has happened in any part of this comedy, that I have gained a turn of style, or expression more correct, or at least more corrigible than in those which I have formerly written, I must with equal pride and gratitude ascribe it to the honour of your lordship's admitting me into your conversation, and that of a society where everybody else was so worthy of you, in your retirement last summer from the Town.' (Jeffares, Vol. 4, p. 109.) His modesty here strongly echoes that of Dryden, who in his celebrated dedication of *Marriage à la Mode* to Rochester similarly maintained: 'I am sure, if there by anything in this play, wherein I have raised myself beyond the ordinary lowness of my comedies, I ought wholly to acknowledge it to the favour of being admitted into your Lordship's conversation. And not only I, who pretend not to this way, but the best comic writers of our age, will join with me to acknowledge, that they have copied the gallantries of courts, the delicacy of expression, and the decencies of behaviour, from your Lordship, with more success, than if they had taken their models from the court of France.' (*John Dryden*, Mermaid Series, ed. Saintsbury, Vol. 1, p. 229.)

The next two centuries saw very few performances of Congreve's plays. The vogue for sentimental comedy in the eighteenth century and the prudery of the Victorian age were equally hostile to the frank quality of his finest work. But when *The Way of the World* and *The Old Bachelor* were revived in the 1920s their refinement of witty dialogue was relished by a more sophisticated society, and they strike a chord again with our more cynical post-war generation. It is interesting to note in conclusion, however, that Congreve himself was so disillusioned by the poor reception of his play in 1700 that he gave up writing for the stage altogether. The times were changing, and both on account of its complex presentation of human relationships and its uncompromising attitudes to money, sex, friendship and marriage the play was disliked. It remains, however, our most complete and subtle comedy of manners, and a reminder that essentially this genre begins where Shakespeare and his contemporaries end: with marriage.

3
The eighteenth and nineteenth centuries

> Plays, I must confess, have some small charms, and would have
> more, would they restrain that loose encouragement to vice, which
> shocks, if not the virtue of some women, at least the modesty of all.
> (Richard Brinsley Sheridan, *A Trip To Scarborough*, 1777)

> It will at any rate hardly be questioned that it is unwholesome for
> men and women to see themselves as they are, if they are no better
> than they should be: and they will not, when they have improved in
> manners, care much to see themselves as they once were.
> (George Meredith, *An Essay On Comedy*, 1877)

The eighteenth century

In the *Spectator* of Tuesday 15 May 1711 (No. 65) Steele
wrote:

> The seat of wit, when one speaks as a man of the town and
> the world, is the playhouse ... The application of wit in the
> theatre has as strong an effect upon the manners of our gen-
> tlemen, as the taste of it has upon the writings of our
> authors.

He proceeded to analyse *The Man of Mode*, concluding:

> This whole celebrated piece is a perfect contradiction to
> good manners, good sense and common honesty; and there
> is nothing in it but what is built upon the ruin of virtue and
> innocence ... To speak plain of this whole work, I think
> nothing but being lost to a sense of innocence and virtue can
> make anyone see this comedy without observing more fre-

quent occasion to move sorrow and indignation, than mirth and laughter.

This criticism is entirely characteristic of the eighteenth century's attitude to the comedy of the Restoration; and it is an approach which is borne out equally in the dramatic writing of the period.

Steele himself was the leading comic dramatist in the first quarter of the century, and one of his early plays, *The Tender Husband* (1705), perfectly illustrates the nature of the sentimental comedy which soon established itself in the reign of Queen Anne. The opening line of the play, 'Well, Mr Fainlove, how do you go on in your amour with my wife?', holds considerable Pinteresque promise; but this is not fulfilled. Fainlove is in fact a woman, the mistress of Clerimont, who is using her in a stratagem to win back his wife. The full consequences of this are seen at the climax of the play (V,i) when Clerimont emerges from hiding to accuse his wife of infidelity. 'Ha, Villain! Ravisher! Invader of my bed and honour, draw', are his first words to Fainlove; they are empty and melodramatic because there was never any real danger of Mrs Clerimont's adultery. She has told Fainlove she considers him 'no more than a thing . . . proper for hours of dalliance . . . [no] competition with a man whose name one would wear'; and the effect of her husband's revelation of the real nature of her 'pretty beau' results in a tearful repentance:

> Oh! look at me kindly — you know I have only erred in my intention, nor saw my danger till, by this honest art, you had shown me what 'tis to venture to the utmost limit of what is lawful. You laid that train, I'm sure, to alarm not to betray my innocence — Mr Clerimont scorns such baseness! Therefore, I kneel, I weep, I am convinced.
>
> (*The Tender Husband*, V,i, Bell's British Theatre, Vol. 8, p. 63)

The key phrase, which reveals how the eighteenth-century

dramatists were to take the sting — and with it the life — out of the comedy of manners is 'I have only erred in my intention'; but the morality of a writer who can fully condone the husband's adultery as part of his 'honest art', and abruptly consign the rejected mistress to the country oaf, Humphrey Gubbin, does not bear close scrutiny.

Though Steele's early plays were an awkward attempt to reflect the manners and morality of the new century, by the time he came to write *The Conscious Lovers* in 1722 he had learnt how to combine a witty style with a sentimental romanticism and thus cater to the tastes of the emerging bourgeois audience. His purpose is stated clearly in the Prologue, where he 'aims to please by wit that scorns the aid of vice', and adds:

> No more let ribaldry with licence writ
> Usurp the name of eloquence or wit . . .
> 'Tis yours, with breeding to refine the age,
> To chasten wit and moralize the stage.

> (*The Conscious Lovers*, ed. Jeffares, Vol. 4, p. 517)

The desire to 'moralize the stage' in the eighteenth century sprang from a different source from that which resulted in the religious bigotry and psychological repression of the Victorian period: it proceeded from a belief in reason and good nature as the guiding principles of human conduct. Thus when Bevil Junior informs his friend Myrtle that he has no interest in Lucinda, Myrtle replies:

> There you spoke like a reasonable and good natured friend. When you acknowledge her merit, and own your prepossession for another, at once, you gratify my fondness, and cure my jealousy.

> (*Ibid*, II,i, p. 538)

Nothing could be further from the standards of the previous age: precisely because the crucial issues of friendship, sex and money are treated with such disinterest on the part of the characters, the playwright's manipulation of events may be defined as sentimental. Neither emotion nor reason governs the action of the lovers. There is a complete lack of self-interest in Bevil's support and protection of Indiana, since he thinks her penniless, but it is duty to his father which deters him from entertaining any hope of marriage. Loyalty also determines his conduct to his friend whose gratitude for persuading him to avoid a duel over Lucinda is significant: 'Dear Bevil, your friendly conduct has convinced me that there is nothing manly but what is conducted by reason and agreeable to the practice of virtue and justice' (*ibid*, IV,i, p. 568). Psychological truth has been sacrificed to prescribed patterns of theatrical behaviour.

It is entirely consistent with such an approach to human conduct that the eighteenth century should have found the escapism of sentimental romance more congenial than the hard facts of reality. Thus *The Conscious Lovers* ends with the revelation that Indiana is the long-lost daughter of the wealthy merchant, Mr Sealand, and consequently heiress to a vast estate. The fact that the play's dénouement is a far cry from anything in Wycherley or Congreve is emphasized by Bevil's acceptance of the situation: 'I hear your mention, Sir, of fortune, with pleasure only, as it may prove the means to reconcile the best of fathers to my love' (*ibid*, V,iii, p. 587). This outcome, which gives the lie to the scepticism of Isabella as well as showing the ambitions of the mercenary suitor, Cimberton, mocked and confounded, is seen as 'the sport of nature and fortune'. Steele is here in the tradition of Vanbrugh and Farquhar, but the more pronounced escapism of his work reflects the tastes of the new bourgeois audience presented sympathetically in the play through the character of Mr Sealand. In his confrontation with Sir John Bevil, Mr Sealand speaks up for his class:

> Sir, as much a cit as you take me for, I know the Town and the world — and give me leave to say, that we merchants are a species of gentry, that have grown into the world this last century, and are as honourable, and almost as useful, as you

landed folks, that have always thought yourselves so much
above us).

(*Ibid*, IV,ii, p. 570)

It is not surprising that an audience composed of such men
would be less interested in the sexual exploits and marital
games which were the privilege of a wealthy leisured aristoc-
racy, and at the same time be unwilling to confront in the theatre the mercantile issues with which they themselves were all
too familiar. Their predilections were to determine the development of the comic drama as the new century developed.

The first indications of this changing shift of values was
shrewdly perceived at the end of the previous century by Colley
Cibber. His play *Love's Last Shift* (1696) provoked Vanbrugh
to a sequel, *The Relapse*, in the same year; and since Vanbrugh's play was adapted by Sheridan as *A Trip to Scarbor-
ough* in 1777 the three dramas provide us with a
comprehensive picture of the change in theatrical taste which
began at the turn of the century. Cibber, aware of the *mores* of
a Protestant court and a less aristocratic audience, makes his
rake, Loveless, repent in the last act. Thus, though he admits
his hero is 'lewd for above four acts', he boasts that 'there's not
one cuckold made in all his play'. This is brought about
through the 'last shift' of the title, another device reminiscent
of Pinter, whereby a wife attempts to regain her husband's love
by offering herself as his mistress. When the trick is disclosed,
Loveless is suitably contrite: 'O I am confounded with my
guilt, and tremble to behold thee', the wife more reminiscent of
Gilbert's Iolanthe as, alternating between 'a fixed posture',
kneeling, falling to the ground and rising, she asks: 'Conscience, did you ne'er feel the check of it? Did it never, never tell
you of your broken vows . . . I am your wife' (*Love's Last Shift*,
V,ii, ed. Jeffares, Vol. 3, pp. 411-8). The hollowness of the feelings here is made all the more evident by contrast with the
play's frankness about sex and money — Young Worthy says

of Hillaria: "'tis a strange affected piece — but there's no fault in her thousand pounds a year, and that's the loadstone that attracts my heart' (*ibid*, I,i, p. 364); and later he comments to Loveless: 'the pleasure of fornication is still the same; all the difference is, lewdness is not so barefaced as heretofore' (*ibid*, III,ii, p. 384).

Vanbrugh's retelling of the story in *The Relapse* achieves a much subtler blend of psychological truth and romantic adventure, though he prepares the way for Sheridan's sentimental treatment of the story. Unlike Cibber, Sheridan is totally consistent to a set of values: by the end of the century there was no attempt to pursue the implications of the sexual intrigue beyond the bounds of strict propriety. Thus Amanda remains faithful to her husband and as a result Loveless does not go through with his seduction of Berinthia. This is as a result of a sequence of highly contrived scenes of eavesdropping, culminating in Berinthia and Loveless hearing Amanda curtly dismiss her would-be lover, which provokes Berinthia's comment: 'Don't you think we steal forth two contemptible creatures?' and Loveless's response: 'When truth's extorted from us then we own the robe of virtue a sacred habit'. (*The Relapse*, V,i, ed. Williams, p. 324). In keeping with Sheridan's more simplistic presentation of the moral issues, Berinthia is not in league with her ex-lover (as in the Vanbrugh play) to effect a double seduction; instead she is angry, and mistaken — in believing that Townly has been false to her — and so turns to Loveless in jealousy and the spirit of revenge. Characters who are drawn in such little depth that they have no existence outside a neatly contrived plot ensure that the audience makes no connection between its own society and the events on stage. We have reached a totally escapist comedy, the opposite of the subversive social satire of the late seventeenth century. Sheridan's dramatic aims are not 'to profit and delight': merely the latter, as the play's conclusion makes clear: 'But of this you may be assured, that while the intention is evidently to please,

British auditors will ever be indulgent to the errors of the performance' (*ibid*, V,ii, p. 332).

The eighteenth-century adaptations of Wycherley's two most celebrated plays also tell us a great deal about the tastes of this new audience. In 1766 Garrick adapted *The Country Wife* as *The Country Girl*. Adultery is completely avoided as the central character, here called Peggy, outwits not her husband, but her guardian, Moody, and marries his nephew Belville. Horner, along with the Fidgets and Squeamishes, is banished from the play. Not surprisingly, Garrick cannot comprehend Sparkish's psychology and has him encourage his rival not out of narcissistic masochism but because 'the more danger, the more honour'. Moody, when finally outwitted, is 'stupified with shame, rage and astonishment' and as he storms off stage Sparkish comments: 'Very droll and extravagantly comic, I must confess!' His remark sums up the tone of the play, which also takes a very sentimental view of money. By marrying against her guardian's will Peggy forfeits half her fortune, but her reaction is entirely characteristic of the eighteenth-century theatre's avoidance of reality in monetary matters, as well as being indicative of the social composition of its audience:

> Great folks, I know, will call me simple slut,
> Marry for love! they cry, the country put!
> With half my fortune I would rather part
> Than be all finery with an aching heart.
>
> (*The Country Girl*, V,ii, ed. Inchbald, pp. 74-5)

The attitude to money in the eighteenth-century drama contrasts sharply with the seventeenth-century view: that marriage is as much a legal and financial settlement as a personal and spiritual union. In Isaac Bickerstaff's rewrite of *The Plain Dealer* (1766) the most careful pains have been taken to tone down the unscrupulousness of the characters in financial affairs. The play is much closer to the original in plot and characterization than is Garrick's revision of *The Country Wife*, and an examination of Bickerstaff's amendments is very revealing. In the first scene between Varnish and Olivia (compare chapter 2, p. 15) Bickerstaff feels compelled to mitigate their treatment of Manly by omitting any mention of the jewels they have stolen from him and by making Olivia sympathetic to Manly's 'present wants' by allowing him some of the thousand pounds he left in her name. Olivia does not rob Plausible and Novel: indeed at the end of the play, rather than being very relieved to regain his wealthy gifts, Plausible is prepared to marry her. Wycherley's deeply serious financial and sexual issues are here lightly dismissed. When Plausible asks, 'Ma'am, will you permit me the honour of your fair hand?' she answers, 'Take it', and strikes him. Olivia is sentimental over Fidelia to the extent of losing interest in money; she offers to put 'a magnificent fortune' into her hands and adds: 'in short I am ready to forsake friends, country, reputation and fly with you'. Similarly Freeman's outmanoeuvring of Mrs Blackacre is tempered with a fascinating addition by Bickerstaff: 'But you shall find I will not be behind-hand with you in *generosity* — I believe I need not tell you, widow, that I have suffered some injuries from your family and there is now an estate in it which *lawfully* and *honestly* belongs to me) (my italics) (*The Plain Dealer*, V,i, Bell's British Theatre, Vol. 31, p. 102). Bickerstaff was attempting in this play to make the actions of Wycherley's savage world fit into a theatrical picture of the society of his own day; that the resultant drama is emotionaly tepid and psychologicaly unconvincing is a reflection both of eighteenth-century social values and of the fact that the stage no longer sought to reflect contemporary *mores* with any real honesty.

Sheridan's two celebrated comedies are a prime example of this. Both *The Rivals* (1775) and *The School for Scandal* (1777) are effectively eighteenth-century impressions of seventeenth-century conduct: in short, pastiches. They are all style without feeling, in much the same relation to the dramas of the post-Restoration period as the operas of Rossini are to those of Mozart. Sheridan professed to set himself against the sentimentality of late eighteenth-century comedy, and thus he parodies conventional romantic attitudes whilst adopting a style imitative of the drama of the previous century. Lydia Languish is ridiculed in *The Rivals* when she utters such remarks as 'How persuasive are his words! how charming will poverty be with him!'; but in his parallels with Wycherley and Congreve, Sheridan is merely superficial. The characters are not drawn in depth, their names — Joseph Surface, Lady Sneerwell, Sir Lucius O'Trigger, Lydia Languish — lack the subtle allusiveness of a Wishfort, Marwood or Pinchwife; everything is spelled out to the audience. In *The Rivals*, I,ii, Lucy confides in soliloquy that she has aided Lydia, betrayed her to Mrs Malaprop, pretended to help both Acres and Sir Lucius, and thus made money out of all of them. Her disarming frankness puts the audience at ease and makes a strong contrast with the way Mirabell manipulates Foible and Waitwell to his own ends. The attempt of the young lovers to outwit Mrs Malaprop is a further borrowing from *The Way of the World*, but the observation of the cunning ruthlessness of the characters in Congreve gives way in Sheridan to the farcical situation comedy of IV, ii, at the end of which Mrs Malaprop accepts Sir Anthony's advice to 'forgive and forget'.

In both *The Rivals* and *The School for Scandal* disguise is basic to the action. Captain Absolute masquerades as Ensign Beverley to pander to Lydia's romantic yearnings for a poor lover (conduct precisely opposite to that of characters like Aimwell and Archer); Sir Oliver Surface pretends to be the poor Mr Stanley in order to test the mettle of his nephews. This sort of disguising, as distinct from the dissimulation basic to the conduct of Restoration rakes and fortune-hunters, means that Sheridan's concerns are more external: the result is situation comedy, not comedy of manners. Significant issues — marriage, adultery and money — are laughed aside: Charles Surface's whimsical refusal to sell his uncle's portrait ensures that he is made inheritor; we are more absorbed by the escalating difficulties imposed on Joseph Surface in the 'screen' scene (IV,iii), of *The School for Scandal* than by any implication or danger of adultery. Indeed, Joseph's pursuit of Lady Teazle has been sexually disinterested from the start. She tells him 'I admit you as a lover no further than fashion requires' and he retorts: 'True — a mere Platonic cicisbeo, what every wife is entitled to' (*The School for Scandal*, II,ii, ed. Williams, p. 190); there has never been any real threat of infidelity, and she returns dutifully meek and contrite, like Steele's Mrs Clerimont, to her husband. Sheridan does not examine their marriage honestly: the conclusion of their argument in II,i makes it clear that they are as ill-matched as Pinchwife and Margery:

> *Sir Peter*: Zounds! madam, you had no taste when you married me!
>
> *Lady Teazle*: That's very true indeed, Sir Peter! and after having married you I should never pretend to taste again, I allow. But now, Sir Peter, since we have finished our daily jangle, I presume I may go to my engagement at Lady Sneerwell's.

> (*Ibid*, II,i, p. 183)

but both Lady Teazle's heavy-handed repetition of the joke and her perfunctory way of ending the argument are indicative of the fact that Sheridan is writing for an audience attuned neither to wit nor emotional truth in character portrayal. The issues throughout, both psychological and moral, are stereotyped. Far from avoiding sentimentality, Sheridan anticipates the melodrama of the next century, notably in the dénouement of *The School for Scandal*, in which the villainess storms off stage followed by her accomplice, himself 'confounded', whilst the young lovers fall into one another's arms and the foolish old husband says to them: 'and may you live as happily together as Lady Teazle and I intend to do'.

The other celebrated comedy of the late eighteenth century, Goldsmith's *She Stoops to Conquer* (1773), makes no attempt to ape the style of the previous century and consequently has a warmth and sincerity lacking in the plays of Sheridan. Possessing, along with his other comedy *The Good Natured Man* (1768), some affinities with the drama of Farquhar, Goldsmith's work firmly establishes the supremacy of rural values over those of the metropolis. Mr Hardcastle, who maintains a high standard of behaviour despite immense provocation, is the positive representative of good breeding, whilst his wife, ridiculed for affecting the manners of the town, is the butt of Goldsmith's satire. The title of the play, which could as well apply to the heroine of Cibber's *Love's Last Shift*, yet again draws attention to a surprisingly modern sexual dilemma; but though sensitive in his treatment of young love Goldsmith is interested not in the psychological but the comic potential of Young Marlowe's embarrassment in the company of sophisticated girls. Comedy of situation is fundamental to this play, and both the Marlowe—Kate love scenes and the vindication of the superior manners of Hardcastle are subordinated to this. Just as any complex examination of both sexual and social issues is avoided, so too the subject of money is not treated very seriously. When Miss Neville tells Hastings she is waiting only to secure her jewels he retorts: 'Perish the baubles! Your person is all I desire'; and though she is more practical, pointing out later: 'In the moment of passion, fortune may be despised, but it ever produces a lasting repentance', the way in which the valuable casket of jewels passes farcically from hand to hand throughout the play makes a telling contrast with the vital transactions relating to the 'black box' in *The Way of the World*. The subtitle of the play — *The Mistakes of a Night* — is indicative of the true nature of Goldsmith's play, which may aptly be termed a comedy of bad manners, and as such is an interesting precursor of *Hay Fever* and *Who's Afraid of Virginia Woolf?*

The Nineteenth century

If the comedy of manners became more and more anaemic in the eighteenth century, by the beginning of the nineteenth it was effectively dead. The popularity of action-packed melodrama and sentimental moralizing comedy, both vindicating the conduct of the pious underdog, was totally antipathetic to the wit and frankness of the comedy of manners. The development of the novel in the wake of Richardson and Fielding also meant that an educated audience turned away from the theatre for its entertainment. In 1806 Mrs Inchbald produced an important edition of plays which included revisions of Wycherley and Farquhar, though not without 'unpleasing comments' in the manner of Lady Bracknell. Of the version of *The Beaux' Stratagem* (which omits the whole of the discussion on divorce at the end of Act III) she comments:

> It is an honour to the morality of the present age that this most entertaining comedy is but seldom performed ... in adorning vice with wit, and audacious rakes with the vivacity and elegance of men of fashion, youth at least will be decoyed into the snare of admiration. (p. 3)

whilst of *The Country Girl* she says:

> [Garrick] expunged those parts of it which probably were thought the most entertaining in the age in which it was written, but which an improved taste delicately rejects. The comedy, in its present state, boasts the witty dialogue of former times, blended with the purity and happy incidents, of modern dramas. (p. 5)

Ironically Mrs Inchbald is best remembered as the author of *Lovers' Vows*, the play which so distressed Fanny Price in Jane Austen's subtle examination of social manners, *Mansfield Park*.

In the first half of the nineteenth century there were two major attempts to vindicate the mannered comedy of the late seventeenth century. In 1833, four years before Queen Victoria came to the throne, the last of Lamb's *Essays of Elia* were published, in one of which — significantly entitled *On the Artificial Comedy of the Last Century* — he propounds an original thesis. 'Congreve and Farquhar', he points out, 'show their heads every once in seven years, only to be exploded and put down instantly'; his admiration for these dramas stems from his belief that the world they represent is unreal: 'It is altogether a speculative scene of things which has no reference whatever to the world that is.' Lamb objects to the moral tone of contemporary drama, lamenting the fact that 'in our anxiety that our morality should not take cold, we wrap it up in a great blanket surtout of precaution against the breeze and sunshine,' and argues: 'I am glad for a season to take an airing beyond the diocese of a strict conscience.' (*Essays of Elia*, pp. 165-72). In replying to critics like Coleridge who found these plays 'wicked' and 'viciously indecent' Lamb argues: 'We are not to judge them by our usages . . . there is neither right nor wrong, gratitude or its opposite, claim or duty, paternity or sonship.' Seven years later Leigh Hunt published his *Dramatic Works of Wycherley, Congreve, Vanbrugh and Farquhar*, but this attempt to re-establish the plays did not appeal to Victorian standards of taste and morality. In reviewing this edition at great length in January 1841 Macaulay was quick to point out the flaw in Lamb's argument, which he saw as 'ingenious' but 'altogether sophistical'. He states:

It is not the fact that the world of these dramatists is a world into which no moral enters. Morality constantly enters into that world, a sound morality and unsound morality; the sound morality to be insulted, derided, associated with everything mean and hateful; the unsound morality to be set off to every advantage, and inculcated by all methods, direct and indirect.

(*Critical Essays*, Vol. 2, p. 418)

In fairness to both Lamb and Leigh Hunt, the former's close analysis of the plays centres on Sheridan, whose work perfectly illustrates the justness of his argument, whilst the latter admitted the 'severity of rascality' in Congreve's comedies 'that produces upon many of their readers far too grave an impression'. Revealingly, Leigh Hunt uses here the word 'readers': the Victorians knew next to nothing of the plays in performance; so that it is not surprising to find Meredith in his important essay *On The Idea of Comedy and of the Uses of the Comic Spirit* (1877) dismissing the genre as trivial with a mixture of moral and aesthetic disapproval

> [The] fan is the flag and symbol of the society giving us our so-called Comedy of Manners, or Comedy of the manners of South-sea Islanders under city veneer: and as to comic idea, vacuous as the mask without the face behind it. (p. 17)

Moral objections, such as Macaulay's claim that these plays were 'a disgrace to our language and national character' were one thing; but a far more effective indictment was that of Meredith, shared by a fellow novelist, Thackeray — who bemoaned the 'weary feast, that banquet of wit where no love is' — namely, that the plays were unfunny.

The significant re-emergence of the comedy of manners in the nineteenth century is to be observed not in plays like Boucicault's *London Assurance* (1841), which in tone is Goldsmith sentimentalized and in form a primitive farce anticipating Feydeau and Labiche; nor in the new school of naturalistic drama introduced a little later by Tom Robertson; nor in the social comedies of Pinero and Henry Arthur Jones at the end of the century; but in the more subversive and bitingly satirical work of Gilbert and Wilde. Gilbert had written a series of verse plays in the 1870s — *The Palace of Truth* (1870), *Pygmalion and Galatea* (1871) and *The Wicked World* (1873) — which in their topsy-turvy approach to sacred social and religious values attacked the hypocrisy of Victorian life. But the sharpness of his satire is blunted by the stilted versification of these early plays as surely as by Sullivan's music during their collaboration later in the Savoy operas. In *Engaged* (1877) however, he wrote a stinging attack on the social *mores* of the time which profoundly influenced Wilde. In this play the conventional attitudes to love and friendship as presented in the stock melodramas of the period are subjected to ridicule, since every character in the play places them after considerations of money. Gilbert thus exposes with shocking candour the refusal of society to face its mercenary code of behaviour. Belinda Traherne tells her lover:

> I love you madly, passionately; I care to live but in your heart; I breathe but for your love; yet before I actually consent to take the irrevocable step that will place me on the pinnacle of my fondest hopes, you must give me some definite idea of your pecuniary position. (*Engaged*, I,i, ed. Booth, p. 247)

Though the parody of the romantic love scene in the above passage is amusing, Gilbert's satire in this play is not subtle. It is, however, absolute: the 'villain' Belvawney does everything in his power to frustrate Cheviot Hill's attempts to marry, since by making sure his friend remains single he retains £1,000 per annum from the grateful father; Symperson, who stands to gain this annuity should his nephew marry or die, cheerfully encourages him to commit suicide when his matrimonial plans are frustrated; Symperson's daughter, Minnie, though engaged to Cheviot Hill, quickly drops her claims on him as well as her aimiable façade of girlish innocence when she discovers he is bankrupt; even the ingenuous Scottish rustics learn to play the game when Maggie Macfarlane, on the advice of her solicitor, discovers it is more expedient to sue Cheviot Hill for breach of promise than to insist on a wedding. When, at the end of the century, Wilde combined his own genius for witty conversation with Gilbert's clever inversion of values he produced four comic dramas which were worthy to stand by those of the seventeenth century.

Wilde astutely combined the popular conventions of melodrama with the unfashionable genre of mannered comedy to produce a complex and vitally original theatrical form. By the end of the nineteenth century the intimate apron stage of the post-Restoration period had finally receded completely behind a front curtain; theatres were now very much larger, the auditorium having given way to what was significantly termed the 'spectatory'. Theatrical gesture and expression had to be much larger than life; and it was Wilde who first observed that a heightening of dramatic language was the only way to get through to his bourgeois audience. His paradoxes and epigrams are far more extreme, more outrageous than the witty expressions of Congreve and his contemporaries; the style is hardened, so that instead of the brilliant quick-fire dialogue of Mirabel and Millament we have the self-dramatizing cleverness of Wilde's arrogant poseurs. Because Wilde himself was such a rebel it is not surprising that the conflict between his public and private life should have found expression in the tension between the sentimental effusions of melodrama and the cool poise of sophisticated social repartee.

His first two plays, *Lady Windermere's Fan* (1892) and *A Woman of No Importance* (1893), are both concerned with the familiar melodramatic figure of the woman with a past; but Wilde's work is a far cry from such pieces as *Lady Audley's Secret*, where the moral issues are very clear cut. Both Mrs Erlynne and Mrs Arbuthnot are victims, representatives of Wilde's criticism of a society which hypocritically ostracizes such women whilst exonerating the men who are responsible for their situation. Mrs Erlynne fights with tougher weapons than Mrs Arbuthnot: her blackmail is a more realistic device than Mrs Arbuthnot's emotive pleading since it challenges the double standards of the fashionable world. She is a shrewd observer, realizing that to regain social standing she must play by the rules. Like Lady Bracknell she knows never to 'speak disrespectfully of society. Only people who can't get into it do that'. She is equally aware of the importance of superficial appearances; when Lord Windermere is angry that she has returned to his house she retorts ('with an amused smile'): 'My dear Windermere, manners before morals!' Unlike Mrs Arbuthnot she refuses to 'have a pathetic scene' and her frankness is a means by which Wilde attacks Victorian cant with his biting parentheses and epigrams:

> I lost one illusion last night. I thought I had no heart. I find I have and a heart doesn't suit me, Windermere. Somehow it doesn't go with modern dress. It makes one look old. And it spoils one's career at critical moments. . . . I suppose, Windermere, you would like me to retire into a convent . . . In real life we don't do such things . . . No, what consoles one nowadays is not repentance, but pleasure. Repentance is quite out of date. (*Lady Windermere's Fan*, p. 65)

A more direct critic of English social life is the American heiress Hester Worsley in *A Woman of No Importance*, but whilst Wilde allows her to voice a good number of home truths he is honest enough to show that she is no match for the sophisticated women around her, as this exchange reveals:

Mrs Allenby: Don't you find yourself longing for a London dinner party?

Hester: I dislike London dinner parties.

Mrs Allenby: I adore them. The clever people never listen, and the stupid people never talk.

Hester: I think the stupid people talk a great deal.

Mrs Allenby: Ah! I never listen.

(*A Woman of No Importance*, p. 91)

In the same play Lord Illingworth warns Gerald: 'People nowadays are so absolutely superficial that they don't understand the philosophy of the superficial' and adds: 'Sentiment is all very well for the buttonhole. But the essential thing for a necktie is style. A well-tied tie is the first serious step in life' (*ibid*, p. 115). In the context of the play this seems merely trivial, the more so as Lord Illingworth is cast as the villain in this melodrama and is utterly humiliated by the end. But when Wilde came to write his next play, *An Ideal Husband*, in 1895 he had learnt how to employ both wit and the structure of melodrama to a more positive critical end. The play is much more honest in following its issues through to their ultimate conclusion. The truth about Mrs Erlynne's real identity remains a mystery to Lady Windermere, nor is she forced to be honest with her husband, as Lady Chiltern in *An Ideal Husband* is obliged to come to terms with her husband's shady past. The subject of this play is not sexual but monetary irresponsibility and thus Lord Chiltern is firmly trapped by Mrs Cheveley's blackmail. Wilde confronts society directly and tersely when he has Chiltern say: 'What this century worships is wealth; the God of this century is wealth. To succeed one must have wealth. At all cost one must have wealth', and he matches this with a dazzling display of paradox from Mrs Cheveley which lays bare an insincerity and hollowness in Victorian life:

> *Mrs Cheveley*: Remember to what a point your Puritanism in England has brought you. In the old days nobody pretended to be a bit better than his neighbours. In fact, to be a bit better than one's neighbour was considered excessively vulgar and middle class. Nowadays with our modern mania for morality, everyone has to pose as a paragon of purity, incorruptibility, and all the other seven deadly virtues — and what is the result? You all go over like nine-pins, one after the other. (*An Ideal Husband*, p. 170)

Lord Illingworth's proud boast that 'the future belongs to the dandy' is borne out not by his own conduct but by that of Lord Goring, who under a mask of disinterested affectation takes care of his friends' financial and emotional affairs, finally bringing about a happy resolution. The witty proposal scene, which mingles romance with a shrewd awareness of emotional issues and financial considerations is also more serious than it appears on the surface; in this it echoes that between Mirabel and Millament in *The Way of the World*:

> *Lord Goring*: Of course I'm not nearly good enough for you, Mabel.
> *Mabel*: (*nestling close to him*) I am so glad darling. I was afraid you were.
> *Lord Goring*: (*after some hesitation*) And I'm . . . I'm a little over thirty.
> *Mabel*: Dear, you look weeks younger than that.
> *Lord Goring*: (*enthusiastically*) How sweet of you to say so! . . . And it's only fair to tell you frankly that I am fearfully extravagant.
> *Mabel*: So am I, Arthur. So we're sure to agree.
>
> (*Ibid*, p. 231)

In his final comedy, *The Importance of Being Earnest*, Wilde achieved an even subtler fusion of mannered comedy and melodrama. He went further than Gilbert in turning the conventions of melodrama completely on their head, and in so doing converted the dangerously heavy emotional passages and the far-fetched coincidences typical of the genre into burlesque. By this means he achieved a consistency of tone which he was able to sharpen to an even more pronounced ironic degree. He called the play 'A Trivial Comedy for Serious People', and it is a mistake to underestimate the serious satiric aims of the work. Though it has a superbly well-constructed plot in which every loose end is finally tied up, and though the prevailing style and refinement of high comedy dialogue have been justly praised, this should not distract our attention from the fact that beyond the shimmering superficial level the play explores in depth the three basic themes of comedy of manners: sex, friendship and money.

Algernon and Jack far outstrip any Restoration rake in their unscrupulous conduct to one another, the ties of friendship being of no concern to them in the pursuit of pleasure. Algernon's convenient euphemism 'Bunburying' is matched by Jack's being called by one name in town and another in the country; through both Wilde is giving us a shrewdly accurate picture of contemporary double standards in matters of sexual promiscuity. But above all the play, like Gilbert's *Engaged*, is inexorable in its exposure of the pecuniary motives of the characters. Lady Bracknell is the arch example of the mercenary Victorian matron whose combination of financial acumen and snobbism Wilde both admires and satirizes. She is interested solely in Jack's wealth and social standing as relevant to 'what a really affectionate mother requires', and during the interview scene in Act I Wilde makes it clear that the two considerations are synonymous:

Lady Bracknell: You have a town house, I hope? A girl with a simple unspoiled nature like Gwendolen, could hardly be expected to reside in the country.

Jack: Well, I own a house in Belgrave Square, but it is let by the year to Lady Bloxham. Of course, I can get it back whenever I like at six months notice.

Lady Bracknell: Lady Bloxham? I don't know her.

Jack: Oh, she goes about very little. She is a lady considerably advanced in years.

Lady Bracknell: Ah, nowadays that is no guarantee of respectability of character. What number in Belgrave Square?

Jack: 149.

Lady Bracknell: (*shaking her head*) The unfashionable side. I thought there was something. However that could be easily be altered.

Jack: Do you mean the fashion or the side?

> *Lady Bracknell*: (*sternly*) Both, if necessary, I presume.
> (*The Importance of Being Earnest*, p. 267)

The brilliance of the above dialogue, which repeatedly shifts its focus of satiric attack, should not blind us to the seriousness of either Wilde's social criticism or Lady Bracknell's attitude. The actress must not attempt to guy the character or her point of view. In her autobiography Irene Vanbrugh, who created the role of Gwendolen, tells us that the acting of Rose Leclerc, the first Lady Bracknell, was 'never stagey or exaggerated', and emphasizes the vital importance of adopting a naturalistic style — basic to any comedy of manners performance — when she says: 'I rejoiced in the sparkling wit when I had learnt to speak it as though it came from myself (Irene Vanbrugh, *To Tell My Story*, London, 1948, p. 33). The humour later in the interrogation scene depends on the contrast between the gravity of Lady Bracknell's tone and the apparent triviality of the issues discussed, culminating in the outraged cry when she discovers Jack was found 'in a handbag'. Edith Evans' famous delivery of the word 'handbag' as a prolonged rising hoot of disbelief provided the perfect climax, thereby representing the height of 'camp' acting. The essence of 'camp' behaviour, on stage or off, resides in an exploitation of the disparity between subject and style. The more subtly this disparity is exploited on the part of the performer — the more cleverly, in fact, he maintains the ironic balance between what he is saying and what he knows his audience is thinking — the more his behaviour can be distinguished as 'high' rather than 'low' camp. But 'camp' behaviour, as with any deliberate stylization of conduct, can be either merely empty or charged with emotional meaning and ironic force. The supreme challenge of 'high camp' acting is the tea scene between Gwendolen and Cecily in Act II where the restrained insults are related to the most mundane of social rituals — the taking of tea — but where every polite question and retort stems from emotional doubt and sexual jealousy. This is

Wilde's art at its finest: the struggle between two women, each determined to keep her man, is conducted entirely as a duel of wits in which the conflict is waged across a tea-table and the seconds are a mute butler and footman.

4

The twentieth century

Keeping our distance is the whole secret of good manners; and
without good manners human society is intolerable and
impossible.

(George Bernard Shaw, *The Apple Cart*, 1929)

The inter-war period

The year 1924 marked a watershed in the development
of the comedy of manners: in that year Bonamy Dobrée's pioneer study *Restoration Comedy* was published, *The Way of
the World* was revived by Nigel Playfair at the Lyric, Hammer-
smith, and Coward's first important comedy, *Hay Fever*, was
performed. In a footnote Dobrée, surprised by the success of
the Congreve revival, asked: 'Do we grow civilized?' The
answer is undoubtedly in the affirmative, since by the mid-
1920s a society emancipated from Victorianism by the Great
War and determined to enjoy a life of house parties, cocktails
and jazz had the leisure once again to appreciate the skill and
sophistication of mannered comedy. Coward, Maugham and
Lonsdale were the chief exponents of the brittle new social
drama, whilst Shaw, still the most important serious dramatist, though ostensibly possessing several thematic and stylistic
features of the genre, serves by contrast rather to define its precise limitations. Shaw distrusted superficiality of style and was
little concerned in his plays with the niceties of social manners;
consequently the lightness and wit which characterize the work
of his contemporaries from Wilde to Coward are absent from

his drama. Rather, his main interests are sociological and political: the verbal battles between Tanner and Anne Whitfield in *Man and Superman* (1901-3) are subordinated to a wider evolutionary thesis; in *Major Barbara* (1905) Lady Britomart's affinities with Lady Bracknell in her domineering manner and social snobbery are at once Shaw's answer to Wilde and part of the drama's complex and paradoxical argument; Professor Higgins' obsession with language and expression in *Pygmalion* (1912) furthers the sociological thesis of the work; and the Orinthia episode in *The Apple Cart* (1929) serves to highlight the political issues basic to the play. Both Maugham and Lonsdale were superficially concerned with the behaviour of high society, but both dramatists appear old-fashioned — essentially nineteenth-century — in style and subject matter when compared with Coward. Lonsdale's *On Approval*, which shows a society woman putting her prospective husband to the test on a lonely Scottish holiday, may have seemed daring in 1927, but the play deliberately avoids any sexual encounter; whilst Maugham's savage misogyny vitiates any attempt at real psychological understanding in his work.

It is Coward who emerges as the sharpest chronicler of the social manners of the 'gay' 1920s and 'turbulent' 1930s, as well as proving to be the most original and influential comic writer of the period. *Hay Fever* was not his first play: in the previous year (1923) he had produced *Fallen Angels*, really an extended review sketch, in which two young wives gradually succumb to the influence of drink and in so doing drop the mask of polite decorum to reveal their real emotional selves; and a drama, *The Vortex*. This is not a comedy, though the conversations between Florence's friends, the sincere Helen, the superficial Clara and the bitchy Pawnie (described in the stage directions as 'an elderly maiden gentleman') are the nearest Coward ever gets to the flamboyant verbal manner of Wilde. This play marked the emergence of Coward as the 'angry young man' of his generation, a role in which he revelled. One particular publicity photograph, which made him 'look like a heavily doped Chinese illusionist ... while temporarily good for business, became irritating after a time, and for many years', Coward remarks, 'I was seldom mentioned in the Press without allusions to "cocktails", "post-war hysteria" and "decadence"' (Introduction to *Play Parade*, Vol. 1, p. x-xi). Coward was always a poseur, and in this he closely resembled Wilde, as well as the Restoration beaux who all cultivated sophistication in dress, deportment and expression. For him wit was not an affectation but the natural expression of a complete life-style. He contrived to behave impeccably on stage and off; the knowledge that the sustaining of effortless repartee as complementary to a superbly unruffled demeanour only comes from years of practice made him contemptuous of what he considered the slovenliness of acting and writing in the 1950s. A remark he made when working with Mary Martin on a TV spectacular sums up the profound truth so often lurking behind the apparently trivial paradox: 'The show will be completely spontaneous, the kind of spontaneity I like best, the kind that comes after five weeks rehearsal' (quoted in Dick Richards, *The Wit of Noel Coward*, London, 1962).

Hay Fever is a play very much concerned with acting, with maintaining a pose, as it contrasts the bohemian life of the artistic Bliss family with the more mundane behaviour of their guests. The play is in fact a comedy of bad manners, acutely observant of the *mores* of the 1920s as it sets the flapper, the vamp, the sporty young chap and the respectable businessman against their selfish and overbearing artistic hosts. Coward repeats the device in *Private Lives* where Elyot and Amanda are contrasted with the 'ninepins' Sybil and Victor, and again in *Design for Living* where the central trio are abominably rude to both Ernest and their American guests in the last act. But because the guests are uniformly dull, and though the Bliss family are — to quote Myra — 'artificial to the point of lunacy' our sympathies are inevitably with the cleverer ones. The frightful party game in which anyone can be called upon to do 'quite usual things like reciting "If" or playing the piano' strikes terror into the guests whose discomfort is the subject of our laughter, notably when Jackie proffers 'appendicitis' as a difficult adverb; but this embarrassment is negligible by contrast with the emotional diversions the family proceed to involve them in when the façade of polite gamesmanship has been dropped. The way in which the Blisses employ their guests as puppets in acting out their own emotional tensions strongly anticipates Albee's sport of 'get the guest' in *Who's Afraid of Virginia Woolf?*, though in *Hay Fever* any really unpleasant psychological or sexual consequences are avoided in the comic curtain to Act II, with the result that we are aware rather of Coward's skill in working out so carefully the complex patterns of action in the piece.

Absolute precision is the hallmark of Coward's style. *Hay Fever's* cleverness resides in the organization of its action and the shrewd observation of social behaviour rather than in wittiness of dialogue, though an anecdote relating to the play's triumphant revival in 1964 at the National Theatre with (as Coward put it) 'a cast capable of playing the Albanian telephone directory' is revealing of the author's scrupulous attention to the minutest detail of expression, as well as indicative of his spontaneous wit. Edith Evans as Judith Bliss consistently delivered one line wrongly: instead of saying: 'You can see as far as Marlow on a clear day, so they tell me', she persistently misquoted the central phrase as 'on a very clear day'. Though apparently a trivial error, it annoyed Coward so much that he finally corrected her for the last time, adding 'Edith, on a *very* clear day you can see both Beaumont and Fletcher' (quoted by Sheridan Morley in *A Talent To Amuse*, pp. 370-1).

In *Private Lives* (1930) we first see the real originality of Coward's dramatic style. The balcony scene of Act I is the perfect counterpart to the Lady Bracknell interrogation scene since, though we again are presented with an example of 'camp' dislocation, in this instance the situation is the reverse of that in the Wilde play: here the subject matter is deadly serious, the style of the conversation flippant and cool. Elyot's staccato delivery and Amanda's cultivated nonchalance — both so perfectly tailored to the acting style of Coward and Gertrude Lawrence — mask a depth of real feeling which will finally break through this deft badinage:

> *Amanda*: Don't leave me until I've pulled myself together.
> *Elyot*: Very well. (*There is a dead silence.*)
> *Amanda*: What have you been doing lately? During these last years?
> *Elyot*: Travelling about. I went round the world you know after —
> *Amanda*: (*hurriedly*) Yes, yes, I know. How was it?
> *Elyot*: The world?
> *Amanda*: Yes.
> *Elyot*: Oh, highly enjoyable.
> *Amanda*: China must be very interesting.
> *Elyot*: Very big, China.
> *Amanda*: And Japan —
> *Elyot*: Very small.
>
> (*Private Lives*, pp. 497-8)

But the Coward scene is different from the Wilde in another, more significant way. Whereas the Wilde scene is written in an ornate style, with periodic sentences taking off on long sweeping flights (requiring great skill in controlled modulation from the actor) the Coward dialogue here is terse, the exchanges more often than not mere phrases. This necessitates very careful timing, the ability to phrase longer units of conversation and the maintaining of a precise balance between a brittle tenuous surface and a depth of emotion. Coward's great originality was to pare down comic dialogue to its bare essentials and thus to escape completely from the high-flown rhetoric of Wilde. In so doing he frequently establishes a tension between this skeletal conversation and the characters' real feelings which thereby constitute a powerful subtext. This is clearly illustrated by a passage from *Shadow Play*, one of the nine short pieces constituting *Tonight at 8.30* (1935) in which a husband and wife, contemplating divorce, look back to the memory of their first meeting:

Vicky: What do you do?
Simon: I'm in a bank.
Vicky: High up in a bank? Or just sitting in a cage totting up things?
Simon: Oh, quite high up really — it's a very good bank.
Vicky: I'm so glad.
Simon: How lovely you are.
Vicky: No, no that came later — you've skipped some.
Simon: Sorry.
Vicky: You're nice and thin — your eyes are funny — you move easily — I'm afraid you're terribly attractive.
Simon: You never said that.
Vicky: No, but I thought it.
Simon: Stick to the script.

(*Ibid*, p. 85)

The brevity of the dialogue, the subtle tension between feeling, thought and speech, and the interpenetration of past and present events strongly anticipate the work of Pinter, notably the Pinter of *Old Times*, whose theatrical technique may also be summed up in Vicky's subsequent line: 'Small talk — a lot of small talk with quite different things going on behind it.'

Coward's originality is seen more clearly by contrast with his contemporaries, Maugham and Lonsdale. It is fascinating to compare the scene between Teddie and Elizabeth in *The Circle* (1921) with the balcony scene in *Private Lives*. In the Maugham play Elizabeth, like Amanda, is contemplating leaving her husband for another man, but the expressions of the young couple here, by contrast with those in the Coward play, appear fulsome and ridiculous. Whereas the conflict between passion and expression gives the Coward characters a fresh- ness and modernity, Maugham's lovers remain products of their own day, quaint examples of a forgotten era:

> *Elizabeth*: Teddie, nothing in the world matters anything to
>   me but you . . . I'll go wherever you take me. I love you.
> *Teddie*: (*All to pieces*) Oh, my God!
> *Elizabeth*: Does it mean as much to you as that? Oh Teddie!
> *Teddie*: (*Trying to control himself*) Don't be a fool, Eliza-
>   beth.
> *Elizabeth*: It's you're the fool. You're making me cry.
> *Teddie*: You're so damned emotional.
>   (*Collected Plays of W. Somerset Maugham*, p. 43)

If Maugham's characters wear their heart on their sleeve, the opposite is true of Lonsdale's. A cultivation of heightened epigrammatic speech distinguishes the figures in his plays, plac- ing him firmly — and derivatively — in the tradition of Wilde. The butler, Charles, making one of his many pointed resumés of the guests in the first scene of *The Last Of Mrs Cheyney* (1925) informs the footman, William:

> He's my lord Dilling. Young, rich, attractive and clever!
> Had he been born a poor man, he might have died a great
> one! But he has allowed life to spoil him. He has a reputa-
> tion with women that is extremely bad, consequently as
> hope is a quality possessed by all women, women ask him
> everywhere. I would describe him as a man who has kept
> more husbands at home than any other man of modern
> times.
>   (p. 12)

Had it not been for Coward, the comedy of manners in the inter-war period would have been stifled under the combined weight of Maugham's gauche emotional effusions and Lons- dale's stale paradoxes.

Coward's finest play is *Design for Living* (1932), because in this work he goes beyond the 'sound sex psychology' underlying the behaviour of Elyot and Amanda to explore in fuller emotional depth but with no loss of wit a complex *ménage à trois*. Gilda, Otto and Leo, after several years spent in a vain attempt to conform to sexual convention, finally realize that they cannot be separated; this occurs at the end of the play when the two men return from their cruise together round the world to reclaim Gilda. Because of the presence of Gilda's guests, none of them will admit to their real desires on this overwhelming occasion; instead they resort to polite conversation in an attempt to hide what they are feeling, so that the whole scene is charged with suppressed emotion which finds expression in oblique references and ironic remarks scarcely perceptible at first to the outsiders. As the psychological tensions increase under the pressure of prescribed etiquette the guests begin to feel the strain until even their social poise is undermined and they leave. Whilst illustrating a highly unconventional approach to friendship and sexuality — which are here seen to be interdependent — this play is Coward's fullest analysis of the career drive. Each character in turn achieves artistic and commercial success — first Leo, then Otto, finally Gilda; and it is not until they are all financially well established that their mutual relationship enjoys an equivalent security. This, Coward's longest and most deeply-felt comedy, fully counters the recurrent charge that his plays are 'thin'. Having established that he could present such complex emotional entanglements whilst maintaining throughout such an acuteness and sophistication of style, he could afford to let his dramatist Leo boast: 'I shall write fat plays from now on.'

Coward continued to write for another thirty years, though he never again returned with such skill to the comedy of manners genre. His greatest successes were henceforth to be broader comedies, plays like *Present Laughter* (1939), which deals with the farcical domestic entanglements of another writer, Garry Esseldine; or *Blithe Spirit* (1941), a more whimsical comedy of situation in which a marriage is quite literally disturbed by a ghost from the past. Pinter's direction of this play at the National Theatre in 1976 brought out all its wit and economy of verbal expression whilst illustrating the affinity between the two dramatists.

If Coward has influenced Pinter in style he has influenced another contemporary dramatist, Alan Ayckbourn, in form. Ayckbourn has proved himself a clever observer of social snobbery within the different levels of the middle class, but his greatest debt to Coward is in the ingenious construction of his dramas. Taking his cue from *Hay Fever* and *Design for Living* he has extended the cunning symmetry of these works so that one play, *How the Other Half Loves* (1970) takes place simultaneously in two socially contrasted households; another, *Absurd Person Singular* (1972), sets its three acts in the kitchens of contrasted homes on Christmas Eve; whilst the action of each part of his trilogy *The Norman Conquests* (1974) is situated in a different room of the same house so that the events of one weekend can be observed from three contrasted viewpoints. As yet Ayckbourn has not combined in one work the central subjects of sex and money but both issues are basic to his unsparing critique of bourgeois behaviour.

Coward wrote no major plays after the war; he was out of sympathy with the age. Dobrée's pioneer study was severly discredited in an important essay by L.C. Knights which first appeared in *Scrutiny* in 1937 and which subsequently proved more influential. Whilst Dobree had stressed the realism of seventeenth-century comedy in contrast to Lamb's extenuation, and countered the Victorian objection to its depravity by arguing that the dramatists were 'trying to rationalise human relationships', Knights argued that 'the trouble is not that the Restoration comic writers deal with a limited number of themes but that they bring to bear a miserably limited set of attitudes', and concluded: 'the criticism that defenders of Restoration comedy need to answer is not that the comedies are immoral but that they are trivial, gross and dull' (see Loftis, pp. 3-21). If Lamb, according to Dobrée, had tried 'to save exquisite work from the oblivion to which an ignorant Grundyism would have consigned it', Knights, enforcing the tyranny of left-wing dogma, attempted to discredit it again. Twenty years later John Wain, sympathetic to Knights' argument that the fault of this dramatic genre essentially resides in its being representative of an 'upper class culture', was to compare Congreve's plays unfavourably with *Charley's Aunt*. This seemed to be the final word, and though the barrenness of English drama in the decade following the war was followed by a profusion of important new plays in the late 1950s, the vogue for realistic theatre with working class settings was even more antipathetic to the comedy of manners. In a period of earnest political and social commitment any undue concern with style was suspect. But ten years later the fashion changed again. In the mid-1960s, as several of the major new authors, notably Orton, Osborne and Pinter, discovered a new refinement of expression, a rebirth of comedy of manners coincided with a significant reappraisal both of Coward and of the dramatists of the post-Restoration period.

Pinter

Of all the new dramatists who emerged in the late 1950s, Pinter is the one Coward from the start most admired. Whilst Osborne's tendency towards rhetoric and his predilection for epigram place him in the tradition of Wilde, Pinter's remorseless paring down of language and economy of dramatic means give him closer affinities with Coward. From his first play, *The Room* (1957), precision has been the hallmark of his style, and he has shown an uncanny ear for dialogue which has led to the suggestion that he must have a tape recorder in his head. John Russell Taylor has expressed this facility for representing everyday speech on stage by saying that Pinter's language is

like ordinary conversation under a microscope. Pinter, however, unlike a more conventionally naturalistic dramatist such
as David Storey, is not concerned to make his characters speak
in such a way that we 'suspend disbelief' and accept their conversation as spontaneous and ordinary. Rather, the resem-
blance to everyday speech forces itself on our attention with
the result that a distortion in the writing and a dislocation in
our approach to it charges the situations, even in his earliest
plays, with elements of both comedy and menace. As he has
developed, Pinter has gradually refined these two features by
placing the tensions and threats more directly in the personal
relationships of lovers, friends, husbands and wives, whilst he
has sharpened the humour, relating the wit to the struggles
involved in an intense verbal gamesmanship. In these respects,
therefore, he has moved away from comedy of menace to
comedy of manners, and this development has been emphasized all the more by the corresponding shift in social environment from the working-class world of the early plays to the
upper-middle-class setting of *Old Times* and *No Man's
Land*.

The Collection (1961) marked an important new step. It was
Pinter's first TV play, his first middle-class drama, his first
comedy of manners. The menacing threats of his earlier work
are also there: the mysterious late night telephone call, the
intrusion of a stranger into a calm domestic situation; but this
drama manifests a sophistication which is in keeping with the
social upgrading of the piece and the intimacy of the new
medium. *The Collection*, as its punning title suggests, is concerned not only with Harry's antiques but also with two cou-
ples whose lives clash, and with a clothes collection shown
in Leeds and the apparently contradictory stories about what
happened between Stella and Bill there. Pinter is dealing here
with a basic theme of most of his works: that the truth is relative — the collection of stories, all different, constitutes a complex picture; but he is not saying that all the versions of the
incident are equally credible. Truth (with a capital T) is a nebu-

lous concept, but one can reach some approximation of it by careful attention to language, expression, style, tone of voice. Pinter reveals that people believe what they like and for them that becomes, indeed is, the truth. He defines this more clearly in *Old Times*, where radical disagreements about the same incidents are qualified by a twenty-year time gap and the subsequent tricks played by memory; in this play Anna says: 'There are some things one remembers even though they may never have happened. There are things I remember which may never have happened, but as I recall them, so they take place' (pp. 31-2). This has a powerful echo of Coward's *Shadow Play*, though Pinter explores the ambiguities and jealousies which arise from sexual misunderstanding and duplicity with a more marked existential emphasis.

In *The Collection*, as with all Pinter's drama, it is not what a character says but how he says it that is most important and revealing. James, in an attempt to bully the truth about his wife's infidelity out of Bill, says:

> You met her at ten o'clock last Friday in the lounge. You fell into conversation, you bought her a couple of drinks, you went upstairs together in the lift. In the lift you never took your eyes from her, you found you were both on the same floor, you helped her out by her arm. You stood with her in the corridor, looking at her. You touched her shoulder, said good night, went to your room, she went to hers, you changed into your yellow pyjamas and black dressing gown, you went down the passage and knocked on her door, you'd left your toothpaste in town. She opened the door, you went in, she was still dressed. You admired the room, it was so feminine, you felt awake, didn't feel like sleeping, you sat down on the bed. She wanted you to go, you wouldn't. She became upset, you sympathized, away from home, on a business trip, horrible life, especially for a woman, you comforted her, you gave her solace, you stayed. (*The Collection*, p. 20)

The coolness of the style here, the neat short phrases in the manner of a police statement, are at odds with the emotive nature of the subject matter, telling us more about James than Bill. Jarring details, such as the yellow pyjamas, the black dressing gown and the toothpaste point to James's desire to paint Bill as a modern Lothario, at the same time setting up a humorous tension which is emphasized by the use of the word 'solace' at the end of the speech. Pinter has a knack of using words which because they are odd, old-fashioned or inappropriate in the mouth of the speaker stigmatize his insincerity or cunning. He makes a similar play with the words 'lest' and 'gaze' in *Old Times*, though the characters in this later play are shrewd enough to spot such tones of voice and use them to their own ends. It is a further inheritance from Coward, another writer acutely conscious of colloquial usage and the implications of every word, as he reveals in *Design For Living* when Gilda, reacting to a review of Leo's play which says: 'the dialogue is polished and sustains a high level from first to last and is frequently witty, nay, even brilliant', has only to comment 'I love "nay" to expose the hollowness of the writer' (p. 374). When Bill is finally goaded into a response his admission, punctuated by pauses and such expressions as 'the truth is', ' I can assure you', 'actually', 'I don't know', 'anyway', 'and that was that', reveals that he is very ill at ease and thus makes his story suspect. Throughout the play the conflicts are entirely verbal: the characters fight only with words; such props as an olive, a drink or a cheese knife being more of a reminder that social decorum is being observed than any real threat of physical violence. James is playing an emotional game with Bill much as he does with Stella later when he implies that he might steal Bill from her. He is in many ways a precursor of Lenny in *The Homecoming*, able to manipulate ideas and objects with equal subtlety in an attempt to gain control and mastery in relationships. But he is defeated as inevitably by a woman who recognizes, as does Kate in *Old Times*, that the best and subtlest weapon in this battle of wits is silence.

The opening conversation of *The Lover* (1963), with its apparently cool acceptance of adultery, establishes a forceful parallel with the attitudes and manners of the Restoration:

> *Richard*: (*amiably*) Is your lover coming today?
> *Sarah*: Mmnn.
> *Richard*: What time?
> *Sarah*: Three.
> *Richard*: Will you be going out ... or staying in?
> *Sarah*: Oh ... I think we'll stay in.
> *Richard*: I thought you wanted to go to that exhibition.
> *Sarah*: I did, yes ... but I think I'd prefer to stay in with him today.
> *Richard*: Mmn-hmmn. Well, I must be off.
> *Sarah*: Mmnnn.
> *Richard*: Will he be staying long do you think?
> *Sarah*: Mmmmnnn ...
> *Richard*: About ... six, then.
> *Sarah*: Yes.
> *Richard*: Have a pleasant afternoon.
> *Sarah*: Mmnn.
> *Richard*: Bye-bye.
> *Sarah*: Bye.
>
> (*The Lover*, pp. 49-50)

The style here is more extreme, however, than anything even in Congreve, the distillation of language to its most basic elements being in marked contrast to the potentially emotive nature of the subject. The little game Richard and Sarah are playing here is developed much more as the play unfolds. Later in the act they discuss their respective lover and mistress openly and with an acuteness of witty observation:

> *Richard*: What does he think of your husband?
> (*Slight pause*)

Sarah: He respects you.

(*Pause*)

Richard: I'm rather moved by that remark, in a strange kind of way. I think I can understand why you like him so much.

Sarah: He's terribly sweet.

Richard: Mmn-hmmnn.

Sarah: He has his moods of course.

Richard: Who doesn't?

Sarah: But I must say he's very loving. His whole body emanates love.

Richard: How nauseating.

Sarah: No.

Richard: Manly with it, I hope?

Sarah: Entirely.

Richard: Sounds tedious.

Sarah: Not at all.

(*Ibid*, p. 61)

The pair sound very much like Elyot and Amanda, but Pinter has an even more serious purpose than Coward. When he springs his *coup de théâtre* at the end of the act in revealing that husband and lover are one and the same person, this places all their previous conversations in a new perspective which throws into relief the more serious game Richard will play in Act II. By the end of Act I Pinter has taken us two stages beyond the conventional marital situation; in the second act he will go further, as Richard forces Sarah to accept the full implications of her femininity. Much as George in *Who's Afraid of Virginia Woolf?* kills the 'child', Richard here kills the 'mistress': she is too conventional, and Sarah must be forced to accept more fully her triple role as whore, mistress and wife by not confining their love-making to the afternoon and by bringing it more openly into the cosy marital context of the evening. Hence the midday sexual diversions, acted out with costumes and the blinds drawn, must become a more integrated part of the relationship. Sarah is unwilling to accept this at first; she realizes the consequences of the new game Richard is playing when he says he has 'paid off' his mistress because she is 'too bony' and she panics:

> *Sarah*: You paltry, stupid! Do you think he's the only one who comes! Do you? Do you think he's the only one I entertain? Mmmnn? Don't be silly; I have other visitors, all the time. When neither of you know, neither of you. I give them strawberries in season. With cream. Strangers, total strangers. But not to me, not while they're here. They come to see the hollyhocks. And then they stay for tea. Always. Always.

(*Ibid*, p. 83)

The strawberries, the cream and the hollyhocks have more than a bawdy significance here; they have all been the subject of conversations earlier, and the reason for introducing John the milkman now becomes clear. Sarah's scene with him gives the lie to the above speech: we know she is faithful to Richard, and she finally accepts his alteration of the rules. In terms of style and manners this play marks a new step for Pinter: nothing that is said can be taken solely at its face value; a complex ritual is gradually refined throughout until the whole drama takes on the force of a powerful image which subtly defines the perfect marital relationship.

Pinter's exploration of the comedy of manners genre had to wait until 1965 before it found expression in a stage work. Prior to this, as well as writing the two plays for television discussed above, he collaborated for the first time with Joseph Losey on the film of *The Servant* (1963). This proved to be the start of a fruitful artistic relationship between the two men, both critics of social behaviour and stylistic perfectionists in their analysis of psychological motivation. Robin Maugham's story *The Servant*, with its exploration of the unscrupulous rise of Barrett, the 'gentleman's gentleman' appealed to Pinter, who in the film presents the power struggle through a series of carefully calculated games by which the servant gradually exchanges roles with his bored, empty-headed and unsuspecting employer. Gamesmanship and love of sport are rarely absent from Pinter's work: for him they represent a code of conduct and a way of exploiting the subtle tensions within society. Sports feature in the other films made with Losey: the violent traditional public school ritual at Lord Cedrington's country house described as 'a murderous game' by Stephen in *Accident* (1967); the country cricket match in *The Go Between* (1971); moreover, in each instance the ostensibly harmless pastime is charged with a wealth of social and sexual significance.

Pinter's last three full-length stage plays, *The Homecoming* (1965), *Old Times* (1971) and *No Man's Land* (1975), reveal a parallel interest in the playing of deadly serious social games according to carefully defined rules. *The Homecoming* explores the clash of values when Teddie, now a lecturer at an American university, returns to visit his aggressively working-class family. The setting, 'an old house in North London', reverts to the lower-class *milieu* of Pinter's earlier works such as *The Room* or *The Caretaker*, but the characters now are very much more articulate. For this reason Lenny's first confrontation with Ruth, though taking place in the early hours of the morning, translates its subdued menace into a verbally pointed conflict of wills. Though he attempts to make her feel ill at ease by tacitly refusing to accept that she is his brother's wife, she is ruffled neither by this nor by his two extravagant stories — of the prostitute and the woman with the mangle — which are subtly offensive and obtusely threatening. Instead she rises to his first physical challenge when he attempts to remove her glass of water.

> *Lenny*: And now perhaps, I'll relieve you of your glass.
> *Ruth*: I haven't quite finished.

Lenny: You've consumed quite enough, in my opinion.
Ruth: No, I haven't.
Lenny: Quite sufficient, in my opinion.
Ruth: Not in mine, Leonard.
    (*Pause*).
Lenny: Don't call me that, please.
Ruth: Why not?
Lenny: That's the name my mother gave me.
    (*Pause*)
    Just give me the glass.
Ruth: No.
    (*Pause*)
Lenny: I'll take it, then.
Ruth: If you take the glass ... I'll take you.
    (*Pause*)
Lenny: How about me taking the glass without you taking
  me?
Ruth: Why don't I just take you?
    (*Pause*)
Lenny: You're joking.

                    (*The Homecoming*, p. 34)

Here the pauses are as significant as the minimal exchanges between the two; every move is carefully countered, every challenge met. The tension increases pointedly until Ruth wins the round by forcing Lenny to shout at her and thus disturb his father.

This marks the beginning of the conflict for dominance between Lenny and Ruth which is to develop through the play. She is the intruder who threatens the complacent male security of the household by her determination to take over on her own terms. The homecoming is really hers, as she returns to her old way of life, but fortified by the intellectual drive she has acquired from Teddie, she is, like Sarah at the end of *The Lover*, a composite of mother, wife, mistress and whore; and she exploits this emotional, sexual and intellectual superiority to the full. Pinter has precisely identified the three sons as a pimp, a doctor of philosophy and a boxer ('in demolition in the daytime'), but their respective qualities of sex, brain and brawn are seen to be powerless against Ruth's combination of talents. The second act, which opens with an amusing and ironic observation of the men on their best behaviour, attempting to savour the delights of post-prandial coffee and cigars, soon gives way to a more disturbing power struggle which culminates in the dispassionate and euphemistic discussion of the financial arrangements for Ruth's establishment as a prostitute in the West End. She drives a hard bargain whilst coolly accepting the fact that her husband leaves, Sam has a heart attack attempting to stop her, and both Max and Joey are literally brought to their knees: Pinter's uncompromising exposure of the bases of human conduct is deeply disturbing, the more so as Ruth's complete sexual and monetary victory is concluded with a calculated precision reminiscent of the 'proviso' scene in *The Way of the World*. This modern Millamant, however, is more than a match for all her admirers, the strongest of whom can in the end merely accede to her demands.

Lenny: All right, we'll get a flat with three rooms and a bathroom.
Ruth: With what kind of conveniences?
Lenny: All conveniences.
Ruth: A personal maid?
Lenny: Of course.
   (*Pause*)
We'd finance you to begin with, and then, when you were established, you could pay us back in instalments.
Ruth: Oh no, I wouldn't agree to that
Lenny: Oh, why not?
Ruth: You would have to regard your original outlay simply

as a capital investment
(*Pause*)
Lenny: I see. All right.

(*Ibid*, p. 78)

In style Pinter's next play, *Old Times*, is his most sustained example of mannered comedy, though the themes of sexual conquest and friendship are interrelated in a vitally original way. It is the most static of all Pinter's full-length plays to date, consisting of the mere exchange of reminiscences, playful and friendly on the surface though in reality a serious struggle to establish dominance. At one point the characters swap phrases of old songs, but even this ostensibly light-hearted diversion is a means for Deeley and Anna to establish emotional, psychological and sexual claims on Kate. At the centre of the drama is a debate as to whether the husband or the girl friend, the present lover or the old soul-mate, can best know the wife. Consequently every story, every recollection introduced by either Deeley or Anna has to be countered by their rival. As the play develops, these interrelated allusions become more subtle in their application so as to constitute a refinement of verbal gamesmanship reflective of complex emotional issues. At one point Deeley, feeling the need for a more expanded and definitive reference to the past, recalls his first meeting with Kate, 'some bloody awful summer afternoon' in an abandoned 'flea pit' which was showing *Odd Man Out*. Precisely remembered facts (the position of the bicycle shop for example) mingle with more imaginative and salacious details (such as the 'sensual relish' exhibited by one of the usherettes) to create a complex impression; but Anna bides her time and much later attempts to discredit Deeley's story when she launches into this description:

And the Sunday papers! I could never get her away from the review pages. She ravished them, and then insisted we visit that gallery, or this theatre or that chamber concert, but of course there was so much, so much to see and hear, in lovely London then, that sometimes we missed things, or had no more money, and so missed some things. For example I remember one Sunday she said to me, looking up from the paper, come quick, quick, come with me quickly, and we seized our handbags and went, on a bus, to some totally obscure, some totally unfamiliar district and, almost alone, saw a wonderful film called *Odd Man Out*. (*Old Times*, p. 38)

This is a calculated attempt to establish the superiority of the civilized artistic and cultural foundation of Anna's relationship with Kate and thereby to belittle Deeley's masculine pride. Everything leads up to the cunningly timed revelation at the end, but Anna's tone here is over-dramatic: the passage has a breathless haste about it which is rhythmically too contrived, whilst again the telling inclusion of the slightly extravagant expressions — 'ravished', 'in lovely London then', 'we seized our handbags' is Pinter's way of giving an ironic dramatic detachment to the piece. This verbal fencing continues, but gradually, through the conflicting accounts of the incident at the party and, more markedly, through the repeated anecdote of the stranger in the girls' room, sophisticated banter and concerns with social behaviour give way to a more deeply philosophical exploration of the nature of reality. The play ultimately begs the question as to whether Kate and Anna are different facets of the same person, and brings all these issues to a conclusion in the final acting-out of the drama's central and recurrent anecdote. In this way *Old Times*, though essentially cast in the style of a comedy of manners, profoundly enriches the implications and possibilities of the genre.

Pinter's latest play, *No Man's Land*, is also principally concerned with friendship. When, late in life, the acquisition of money brings security and domestic luxury whilst at the same time impotence destroys the sexual urge, the need for good society and reliable friends who share one's values becomes paramount. This play contrasts the companionship Hirst can enjoy in the presence of his contemporary, Spooner, with the security guaranteed by the services of his younger employees, Briggs and Foster. But this contrast is rendered highly ambiguous both by Hirst's equivocal attitude to Spooner and because of the undefined status of Briggs and Foster in the household. Spooner presents himself from the start as a civilized and cultured man, unwilling to break the golden rule of hospitality by imposing on his host; but it is not long before he is saying 'I offer myself to you as a friend'. Hirst does not take him up on this; instead he reacts in an odd manner: falling over, and then leaving the room, only to return and treat Spooner as a complete stranger. This behaviour is contrasted in the second act with his false *bonhomie*, as the two exchange ribald stories as though they were the oldest of friends. These marked changes of attitude are a reflection of the familiar masculine reticence which maintains a number of different subterfuges in an attempt to avoid too close and compromising a relationship; the fact that Hirst has apparently just picked up Spooner on Hampstead Heath only serves to throw this into sharper ironic relief. At the beginning of Act II both boast of their past sexual conquests with an elegance of euphemistic expression: as in Spooner's reference to Arabella Hinscott's 'particular predilection' for 'consuming the male member'. They are playing an even more obtuse game than the characters in *Old Times*, a game which does not admit of a comment such as Anna makes after one of Deeley's boastful sexual anecdotes: 'I've rarely heard a sadder story'. The unwillingness to face the emotional implications of a close male friendship is also manifested in Spooner's insistence on talking about their two wives. His goading of Hirst with the outrageous *double entendres* of his sporting metaphor:

Tell me with what speed she swung in the air, with what

velocity she came off the wicket, whether she was responsive
to finger spin, whether you could bowl a shooter with her,
or an offbreak with a legbreak action. In other words did
she google? (*No Man's Land*, p. 30)

culminates in his challenge: 'I begin to wonder whether you do
in fact truly remember her'. Hirst is no match for Spooner in
his playing of a clever verbal game; the latter with his paradoxical sense of 'truly accurate and therefore essentially poetic definition' bases his conduct on the assumption 'All we have left is
the English language', adding 'Can it be salvaged? That is my
question' (p. 18).

But Spooner has not the assurance and command which his
relentless employment of language seems at first to suggest.
The hollowness of his style is exposed by Briggs and Foster
whose coarseness of expression hints at the violence of their
way of life. The opposition of the manners of the country and
the town in the comedy of the late seventeenth century has
given way here, as in *The Homecoming*, to a conflict of different social classes: Pinter amusingly exploits this clash of contrasted standards of behaviour in the terse exchanges between
Briggs and Foster when Hirst asks them to share an established
upper-middle-class social ritual in drinking with his new
friend.

Briggs: (*to* Foster) Where's your glass?
Foster: No thanks.
Hirst: Oh come on, be sociable. Be sociable. Consort with
  the society to which you're attached. To which you're
  attached as if by bonds of steel. Mingle.
(Briggs *pours a glass for* Foster)
Foster: It isn't even lunchtime.
Briggs: The best time to drink champagne is before lunch,
  you cunt.
Foster: Don't call me a cunt.
Hirst: We three, never forget, are the oldest of friends.

Briggs: That's why I called him a cunt.
Foster: (*to* Briggs) Stop talking.

(*Ibid*, pp. 84-5)

As in the plays of Congreve, Pinter's social satire cuts both
ways: Briggs is shrewd, Foster cunning; both are determined to
protect their interests against an outsider. Like Spooner, Foster is a con-artist, but he is more aware of the tangible material
superiority of the sophisticated life-style to which his looks
give him access. To him the shabbiness of Spooner's appearance is anathema and he retorts with a mixture of coarseness
and refinement:

> You've just laid your hands on a rich and powerful man. It's
> not what you're used to, scout. How can I make it clear?
> This is another class. It's another realm of operation. It's a
> world of silk. It's a world of organdie. It's a world of flower
> arrangements. It's a world of eighteenth-century cookery
> books. It's nothing to do with toffee apples and a packet of
> crisps. It's milk in the bath. It's the cloth bell-pull. It's organi-
> zation. (*Ibid*, p. 49)

Moreover, it is Foster who finally outwits Spooner by catching
Hirst in a semantic and philosophical trap. In twenty years the
original confident assumptions of the new left-wing social
drama have developed into a far more witty and complex theatrical analysis of the class struggle.

Osborne

Because of their concern with wealthy upper-middle-class characters and their emotional restraint reflected in a refinement of
dialogue, Osborne's trilogy, *Time Present, The Hotel in
Amsterdam* and *West of Suez*, which appeared between 1968
and 1971, came as something of a shock. Nothing he had written earlier had quite prepared his audiences for this style of
drama, and since his more recent work has shown a marked

falling-off of quality, these three plays stand firmly apart, revealing most fully his mastery of the comedy of manners idiom. Judging from these dramas — and sequels such as *The End of me Old Cigar* (1975) and *Watch It Come Down* (1975) — it might at first appear that the young rebel of the 1950s has become the middle-aged reactionary of the 1970s, since rather than anger we have irony, instead of a cry for change a contempt for revolution, and in place of an antisocial hero a series of artists passionately concerned to uphold the values of a civilized life.

But this would be to take a very narrow view. Osborne has always been essentially an Augustan writer, and his eighteenth-century affinities are most clearly in evidence in his script for the film of *Tom Jones*, directed by Tony Richardson in 1963. The film captures with equal force the bucolic zest for life of the fox-hunting *bon viveur* Squire Western, and the subtlety of sexual intrigue which centres on the London social circle dominated by Lady Bellaston. Osborne's sympathy with Fielding's world is reflected in the delicious touches he adds throughout the film, such as Miss Western's peremptory dismissal of a country highwayman: 'Deliver! I am no wandering midwife, sir. Deliver what?' (p. 128) or Lady Bellaston's sarcastic observation on Sophie: 'the girl is obviously intoxicated, and nothing less than ruin will content her' (p. 134). The skills of two experienced actresses, Edith Evans (as Miss Western) and Joan Greenwood (as Lady Bellaston), were once again employed in the portrayal of these ladies of fashion. The film celebrates the values, rural and urban, of a civilized English life, and it is precisely because Osborne in the late 1950s felt that the quality of life was being endangered that he lashed out through the characters of Jimmy Porter and Archie Rice. There is much of the rebel in Osborne, but none of the revolutionary: he has never sought to change the framework of society (as have some of his contemporaries, Wesker, Bond — and even Orton) but rather to attack abuses within it; it is not

England he hates but the weaknesses and crimes that make her degenerate; his contempt is not for Colonel Redfern in *Look Back in Anger* (1956) but for cousin Nigel.

At times emotion gets the better of style, notably in the unsheathed savagery of his notorious open letter to England and the crude satire of *The Blood of the Bambergs* (1962), but even these two pieces — the latter a dramatization of a royal wedding in which the princess is obliged to marry a photographer when her fiancé, the homosexual Prince Heinrich, is killed in a car crash — direct their scorn at corrupt politicians and cheap journalists who, like the monarchy, have betrayed an ideal of conduct and style. The regrettable weaknesses of Osborne's most recent plays are also in the main due to an excess of emotional and critical fervour, for ironically he has again shown himself to be guilty of the cardinal sin against which Lamb warns Frederica in *West of Suez*: 'Don't be intemperate; you lose your style.'

The Blood of the Bambergs was performed with *Under Plain Cover* as a double bill under the pointed title, *Plays for England*, and it is in these two plays as well as the significantly named *A Patriot for Me* (1965) that Osborne first reveals indications of a marked sharpening and refinement of ironic dialogue. In these plays we catch a glimpse of the terser and wittier vein of expression that distinguishes the conversations of the characters in his mature dramas, and which has developed from Jimmy Porter's lengthy rhetorical outbursts and the clever music hall patter employed by Archie Rice both on stage and off. Thus in *The Blood of the Bambergs* Brown, after saying to Taft: 'has it never struck you as slightly odd, even for a young Prince, that he should divide his time almost exclusively between the barracks and visiting the ballet?' proceeds to itemize the faults of the women eligible to marry the Prince:

Brown: Mariana?
Taft: Yes, you know, the Stettin-Bambergs.

> *Brown*: Stettin-Bambergs? Nobody will speak to them, even
> in their own country.
> *Taft*: There's always Princess Theresa.
> *Brown*: They couldn't raise enough credit to put a deposit
> on a TV set to watch the wedding . . .
> *Taft*: Have you ever considered Isabella, the Grand Duchess
> of —
> *Brown*: Yes I have. She has to shave twice a day, so she'd be
> able to use the Prince's razor, since he doesn't have to.
> *Taft*: I think that's a very cruel, distasteful thing to say.
>
> (*The Blood of the Bambergs*, pp. 34-5)

Osborne does not here have a complete mastery of this sub-Wildean style: he could, for example, have given more bite to Brown's first remark above by omitting the word 'visiting'; but he is exploring a new idiom. *Under Plain Cover* is considerably more successful, as in this play he forges a genuinely witty and original dialogue — a combination of Restoration bawdy and quick-fire repartee — to express the complex emotional and sexual relationship of Jenny and Tim. At one point they talk for several minutes about knickers and the invention never flags, either in such exchanges as:

> *Tim*: The Prime Minister's Country House — Seat: Knickers.
> *Jenny*: Of course. Why don't you come down for the weekend?
> *Tim*: Open to the public on weekdays.
> *Jenny*: Until they pull it down.
>
> (*Under Plain Cover*, p. 113)

or in the lengthier flights of rhetoric which both sustain in this subtle erotic game. Osborne's purpose in this play is deliberately subversive: he presents a sado-masochistic (indeed, incestuous) relationship as perfectly acceptable, since this comedy of sexual manners (an interesting parallel to Pinter's *The Lover*) reveals how a clever manipulation of roles in the lovemaking ritual animates and enriches the marriage. The passages cited above may well appear, as Taft puts it, 'cruel and distasteful'; Osborne, like Orton, often goes out of his way to shock. But he makes it clear, notably in *The Hotel in Amsterdam* — which contains witty conversations on such topics as menstruation and the technicalities of homosexual intercourse — that it is not so much the subject-matter as the style of the discussion which is vital.

A play which gave much more offence, however, was *A Patriot for Me*, for the Lord Chamberlain insisted on numerous cuts including the omission of three whole scenes. One of these was the 'drag' ball which opens Act II and which in the printed text is prefaced by a four page discussion of the manner in which it is to be presented, culminating in a lengthy description of the six different types of homosexual who make up the complex social mixture of guests. The Baron Von Epp, 'a discreet drag queen', appears as Queen Alexandra, but 'remains in absolutely perfect taste' throughout. The poised elegance of his snobbery is supremely evident in his verbal display to impress Redl and his new boyfriend, Stefan:

> *Baron*: The Viennese gull themselves they're gay, but they're just stiff-jointed aristocrats, like puppets, grubbing little tradesmen or Jews and chambermaids making a lot of one-two-three noises all the time. Secretly they're feeling utterly thwarted and empty. The bourgeoisie daren't enjoy themselves except at someone else's expense or misfortune ... Poles are fairly gay. You're Polish or something, aren't you Alfred? And somehow they're less *common* than Russians. Serbs are impossible, of course, savage, untrustworthy, worse than Hungarians, infidels in every sense.
>
> (*A Patriot for Me*, pp. 78-9)

His fancy dress costume gives him the privilege and security of a fixed pose which he exploits to the full, though at the end of the conversation he justifies his attitude in a speech which defines the essence of good breeding:

> *Baron*: And do you think I'm a snob?
> *Stefan*: You appear to be.
> *Baron*: Well, of course I am. Alfred will tell you how much.
> However, I'm also a gentleman, which is preferable to
> being one of our dear Burgomaster Lueger's mob. Taste,
> a silk shirt, a perfumed hand, an ancient Greek ring are
> things that come from a way not only of thinking, but of
> being. They can add up to a man.

> (*Ibid*, p. 79)

The play in fact takes an issue basic to the comedy of manners
— the conflict between passion and the strict code of behaviour society forces on the individual — and gives it precise definition in relation to the social problems of the homosexual.
Another scene, Redl's quarrel with his young lover, Victor
(III,v,) in its absolute precision of invective achieves the perfect balance between intellect and emotion which characterizes
the finest dramatic prose of Congreve. Redl's long diatribe,
interrupted only once by Victor's emotive admission: 'I do love
you', has both a terrifying frankness and icy control which is
more impressive than anything in Osborne's earlier plays and
clearly anticipates the subtler manipulation of language in
Time Present, The Hotel in Amsterdam and *West of Suez*.

Time Present, the first of these plays, presents an attitude
which is common to all three: that style, manners and breeding
are the prerogative of a dying class. All the characters in this
trilogy who possess these social graces are, in pointed contrast
to the figures in other plays of this genre, the losers. This makes
Osborne's dramatization of these qualities of refinement more
ambiguous, since the sympathy he feels for those people who
cultivate them, and his parallel contempt for the insensitive
boors who invade their lives, is tempered by the fact that it is
the latter who are happy and successful. Pamela in *Time Present* has a relentless insistence on taste: the list of activities she

regards as 'vulgar' ranges from dieting and smoking pot to getting drunk or having a nervous breakdown. A permanent supply of good champagne is indispensible to her life-style: 'Just good trusty old Moet', as she puts it; Dom Perignon she considers 'very vulgar'. Her trendy younger sister's criticisms merely act as an incentive to her wit, which ranges from the quick snub:

Pauline: You kill me, you're so provincial.
Pamela: Very likely. As your mother will remember, I was born in India.

to lengthier put-downs:

Pauline: Oh, you're just camp.
Pamela: So I've been told. Just like my father. I wish I could say the same for you. It's impossible to argue with someone wearing such cheap clothes. Take a glass of champagne down to Dave. He doesn't *need* to look quite so ugly, you know. I suppose he thinks *he's* beautiful, of course.'

(*Time Present*, p. 25)

Pamela's responses here are quick, sharp and to the point: they contrast markedly with Jimmy Porter's lengthy tirades, though *Time Present* has certain clear resemblances to *Look Back in Anger*, notably in the figure of the adoring friend and the significance of an off-stage death. Just as the funeral of Hugh's mum is for Jimmy Porter a test of the mettle of his wife and friends, so Orme with his carefully calculated style of acting and living represents for Pamela an ideal of behaviour. Significantly, Jimmy is the only person who attends the funeral, Pamela the only person who deliberately stays away from the memorial service; Jimmy measures everyone by the intensity of their emotional commitment, Pamela by their restraint. She tells Constance, 'I think there's a certain grace in detachment', and criticizes her friend's insensitivity to 'tones of voice'. Their discussion on this subject is significant:

> *Pamela*: I think you *should* pay more attention to tones of
> voice. They are very concrete. You have plenty of them.
> *Constance*: You mean I dissemble?
> *Pamela*: I mean you are many things to different people.
> *Constance*: A trimmer?
> *Pamela*: In the House, to your constituency, in the papers,
> on the telephone, in bed; I don't know about that, but
> you're determined not to be caught out. You're deter-
> mined.
>
> (*Ibid*, pp. 43-4)

Pamela is shrewd enough to understand Constance who,
unlike her, possesses those qualities of ruthlessness that guarantee success in both her career and love life. Pamela cannot dis-
semble; like Manly or Alceste, she must speak her mind, and
she is no less bitter than Wycherley's malcontent. Her devastat-
ing attacks on Abigail are both funny and accurate but they
stem, as Edward points out, from 'professional envy'. Though
the play has no plot and the relationships merely break down,
rather than develop, Osborne creates a mounting tension
which arises from the contrast between the slow pace of the
action and the increasing speed with which Pamela drives herself out of the lives of those who care for her. As a lover, wife,
friend and actress she is a failure; wit is no longer for her a
means to an end: the mask of style has frozen into a permanent
attitude which refuses to admit feelings and needs.

Laurie in *The Hotel in Amsterdam* is a similar character, an
aggressive poseur who uses repartee as a dazzling defence to
cover his emotional unhappiness and insecurity. But his more
animated use of language reflects both a deeper sensitivity and
the determination which has guaranteed his commercial success. He is at the centre of a group of six people whose mutual
friendship and conversation serve to define a high level of
social behaviour. A mere glance at the text reveals that

Osborne has created a smooth exchange of brief remarks shared between the six, which is in marked contrast to his previous plays where in each case the leading character, from Jimmy Porter down to Pamela, dominates the conversation. Laurie's four longer speeches: in Italian (p. 100), on K.L. (p. 117), on his relatives (p. 126) and the lengthy joke about the nuns (p. 134) therefore stand out as 'turns', set pieces for the entertainment of his friends. The first and the last are straightforward displays of verbal skill; the other two more complex, for his description of K.L. rapidly develops into a white hot piece of invective holding passionate hatred in tight intellectual control; whilst the piece about his relatives, entertaining and witty though it is, has a subtext of guilt and suffering which produces a far more complex dramatic impression than Jimmy's incessant abuse of Alison's mother in *Look Back In Anger*.

When the play opens, the tone is more urbane. The presence of the disapproving waiter gives rise to a conversation which in its verbal precision and paradoxical argument has a strong echo of Wilde; indeed the waiter, an ancestor of Leroy in *West of Suez* and Wain in *The End of me Old Cigar*, is a descendant of Lane and Merriman from *The Importance of Being Earnest*.

Laurie: Thought you were a bit effeminate, I expect.
Gus: Perhaps he did. I think its these bloody trousers, darling. You said I should throw them away. They don't do much for me do they?
Laurie: Nothing desirable.
Annie: Darling, you always look rather effeminate. You and Laurie both do in different ways.
Gus: Ah, but Laurie carries it off somehow, I don't.
Margaret: Especially to foreigners.
Annie: It's part of your masculine charm.
Gus: What do you mean?
Annie: Oh, I don't know. A kind of mature softness.

Margaret: And peacockery.

(*The Hotel in Amsterdam*, p. 97)

But the unspecified threat this waiter offers to their security is emphasized by the frequency of their references to K.L., the man they cannot forget despite their escape from him. It is, however, given more tangible expression with the arrival of the uninvited and unwelcome guest, Gillian. She cannot make her unhappiness stylish and funny, as Laurie can, and the full force of his pointed sarcasm is reserved for her crude emotionalism, which he finds vulgar and offensive.

Margaret: It's just that she's been having a bad time lately.
Laurie: What bad time?
Margaret: I'm not sure but this affair she's been having —
Laurie: Oh, fleecing another rich duke of £500 and clench-
  ing her fists because she didn't lose her cherry until she
  was twenty-eight and she doesn't think she gives satisfaction and she plays Bach fugues all night and she doesn't
  wash her hair because it's all so difficult. Blimey! I think *I*
  complain. She needs a public recognition for the suffering she undergoes, that's all. Then she'll feel better. She
  could get the Golden Sanitary Towel Award. K.L. can
  give it to her at the Dorchester with all the past winners
  present.'

(*Ibid*, pp. 114-5)

Osborne here achieves a recognizably individual tone of voice for his character whilst making us feel that this attack is spontaneous and yet the product of a man in complete control of his emotions. Later in the play, just before the happiness of the group is finally destroyed, he again fuses all these skills in the poignant scene where Laurie, with all the subtlety of a seventeenth-century beau, choses precisely the right epithets to convince Annie of the sincerity of his declaration of love:

Laurie: Why? Because ... to me ... you have always been

the most dashing ... romantic ... friendly ... playful ...
loving ... impetuous ... larky ... fearful ... detached
... constant ... woman I have ever met ... and I love
you ...
                                                    (*Ibid*, p. 139)

Command of language passes into good breeding when, having elicited a confession of love from Annie, Laurie says: 'So
there it is. It's snowing again ... I wonder what it will be like in
London?' The fellowship that exists between the six friends is
too important for the delicate balance of relationships to be
upset by any selfish or thoughtless conduct.

The sense of a clearly-defined social unit is perceptible also
in *West of Suez*. But the long opening dialogue between Frederica and Edward, interrupted by the menacing figure of Leroy,
defines the subtle tensions and hostilities within their marriage
whilst preparing us for the breakdown of the façade of good
manners, geniality and sophisticated conversation which is a
prelude to the physical violence at the end of the play. In this
work all the characters are measured according to a criterion
of behaviour reflected in speech. Thus when Edward says to
Frederica: 'I've always been prone to being taken in, like a
pussy-cat's laundry', she recognizes the insincerity and comments, 'Now you're straining' (p. 17). The chief arbiter of style
in this play is Wyatt, who has perfected a pleasant, avuncular
manner which masks his real nature. His younger daughters
see through this, just as Pamela sees through Constance:

> *Wyatt*: I wish I noticed things like *you* all do.
> *Mary*: I think you do really, Daddy. You don't miss the
> tricks.
> *Wyatt*: Devious you mean? Yes I see you do. That's not a
> nice trait either. Pretending not to notice, when all the
> time you do.
> *Evadne*: We forgive you.
>
> (*West of Suez*, p. 45)

Wyatt is, like Laurie, the centre of attraction; an older, more urbane, supremely witty raconteur; only later will his true strength of character and determination be seen, when he confronts the local journalist, Mrs James. As the guests arrive at the end of Act I they too are placed in relation to the standards of Wyatt's circle. Alistair, the camp hairdresser, bursts on the company with a deliberate attempt to impress which marks him as the Witwoud of the group; Harry, the laconic American, says little of consequence; Jed, the student, answers Wyatt's pleasant greeting, 'How do you do, Jed. Where are you on your way to?' with one word: 'wherever'; and Lamb, the commercial writer, potentially Wyatt's rival, says no more than is necessary.

Osborne has thus prepared us for what will happen after lunch. As the family and guests return to the loggia and begin to talk, the virtues of good society become clear: civilized conversation is not a mere façade, a surface of polite manners, unrelated to life; it measures and represents the quality of that life. Under the influence of the meal and the company Wyatt briefly drops his ingenuous pose and Robert reveals a crucial insight into Jed, who is significantly absent:

> *Wyatt*: Chatter sins against language, and when we sin against the word, we sin against God. Gosh, I am pompous.
> *Frederica*: I wasn't going to say it.
> *Wyatt*: Must be the Brigadier's cuddly, loving little grape. Where's your old man got to?
> *Frederica*: He's out there on the beach, talking to Jed.
> *Lamb*: Oh, *does* he talk?
> *Robert*: I think there is someone who could sin against language if he could bring himself to it.
>
> (*Ibid*, p. 57)

Soon the calm tone is broken as Lamb and Frederica tussle, and then Wyatt is finally roused by the arrival of Mrs James.

The laconic charm of his previous manner soon gives way to a brilliant countering of the reporter's criticisms, and then an iron control of argument. The pointedness of his early replies has all the confident assurance of dandies such as Wilde or Coward:

> *Mrs James*: What do you think of man?
> *Wyatt*: As a defect, striving for excellence.
> *Mrs James*: Do you really think that?
> *Wyatt*: No, but presumably you want me to say something, however dull. However, I do think that there is a disastrously false, and very modern, idea that you can be absolutely honest.

> (*Ibid*, pp. 71-2)

His most impressive speech is his savage denunciation of critics, which is double effective: as a logical development of the character Osborne has drawn in the play, and as an ultimate comment on the subject of one of the playwright's own *bêtes noires*. Moreover the speech, ending with Wyatt's admission that he fears 'ludicrous death' and 'feel[s] it in the air', anticipates Jed's outburst in the final scene. In contrast to the command of rhetorical invective displayed by Wyatt, Jed's hatred can find no adequate vehicle for its expression. What is so disturbing here is the total collapse of language. Jed's anger is absolute: unlike Jimmy Porter, however, he is a revolutionary. His savage verbal onslaught is both in matter and manner a complete denial of the civilized values represented by Wyatt, and the physical violence manifested in the senseless murder of the artist is its inevitable and instantaneous corollary.

The End of me Old Cigar is important to our study since Osborne has called it (in the programme note to the original production at Greenwich) 'a modern comedy of modern manners'. Act I, essentially a verbal *tour de force* for Regine, Lady Frimley, punctuated by the gradual arrival of her individual guests, has obvious affinities with this genre. Osborne has rarely written such a consistently funny act. Regine's command of language is pyrotechnic, combining epigram, wisecracking rhetoric, and sarcasm to great effect. Her first remarks to Lady Gwen Michelson, 'another nibbling girl-actress who went to Hollywood too late but brought it back to Weybridge or somewhere' are typical:

> Not dieting again. It's so *oppressive*. Like your eye-lashes and wigs. People who diet are like converts to warmed-up religious beliefs. And your lovely rich husband, and various children by which of them and your home? How *is* your home? The Ranch Style one in Mill Hill? Or have you moved?
>
> (*The End of me Old Cigar*, p. 30)

Regine's critique of significant operatic comedies of manners — *Le Nozze di Figaro, Don Giovanni* and *Der Rosenkavalier* — is fascinating, particularly the reference to the trio from *Der Rosenkavalier*, which is presented both here and in Osborne's previous play *A Sense of Detachment* (1972) as a prime example of sophistication in the controlled presentation of complex emotions.

This play's concern with sex and money in the power game also places it in the tradition of Congreve; Regine's sarcastic comment to John Stewkes: 'Power is so sexy, as we all know. Even more than money. I've never had either but I can recognize it, particularly in bed' (p. 40) is complex because she is lying: she is in fact 'a Jewish girl from Hackney' who has exploited several husbands to gain wealth and who is now planning to blackmail the whole male race into subservience with the compromising films she has made of their illicit sexual antics. Her scheme is extravagant and Osborne treats it merely as a peg on which to hang a number of clever caricatures of well-known society figures. The humour in the work stems more from our identifying these satiric portraits than from any observation of the complexities of personal or social motivation; but his success in this area, as well as his employment of Regine as his own mouthpiece, disturbs the central point of the play which emerges clearly in the second scene of Act II.

Here Len and Isabel discover a mutual love for one another; Osborne contrasts Regine's unscrupulous plotting with the tenderness of a real human relationship. The situation is very different from that in *The Hotel in Amsterdam*; here the language of the lovers seems mawkish and contrived, since Osborne is more concerned to use their affair as vindication of his own anti-liberationist argument. As the two 'go hand in hand up centre to the door' Len's final remark, which ends the play, is: 'And always remember, ladies. At least in *your* cases: "A WOMAN IS A WOMAN BUT A GOOD CIGAR IS A SMOKE."' The capital letters and italics are sufficient indication of the clumsiness of Osborne's method, which is even more clearly perceptible in the fact that Regine's plan is defeated by her inferior, Stan — 'rather the sort of man who poses in the nude for magazines or manages pop-groups or boutiques'. This description (confined to a stage direction) reveals Osborne's unconcealed contempt for fashionable trends as well as his inability to give this attitude convincing dramatic shape and force. The 'victory' of the two lovers seems in this light all the more hollow, and there is something both sadistic and salacious in the way Osborne shows his female liberationists gleefully prostituting themselves to the men for a political motive, only to be tricked in the end. But the play's biggest weakness is its inability to establish a positive set of values against which to measure the characters' actions. It is instructive to compare this drama with the mock-heroic poems of Clive James, notably *The Fate of Felicity Fark in the Land of the Media* (London, 1975) for here James presents a similar milieu with a subtler command of language, a sharper accuracy in his satiric vignettes, and more success in presenting a standard by which the achievements of his figures are to be judged. His description of Kenneth Tynan has a two-sided

edge which places his work firmly in the critical tradition of
Dryden:

> Ken Onan's face is grey-blue like a clinker
> And in his lap his boneless fingers tinker
> Dispassionately with his wilting quill.
> He has the gift, alas he lacks the will.
> The Spirit of Right Reason cries 'Come Back,
> The Dunces Reign! Return to the Attack!
> Unseat triumphant Dullness from her saddle
> And put the Fear of Wit in Fiddle-Faddle!
> But nothing takes his eye or primes his pen.
> Most self-delighting and self-damned of men!
>
> (p. 81)

The End of me Old Cigar is the only one of his works which
Osborne has described as a comedy of manners, and indeed the
dénouements of *Time Present*, *The Hotel in Amsterdam* and
West of Suez make it difficult to classify these plays as comedies in any sense except the Chekhovian. Their observation of
the complexities of human motivation and their mixture of the
tragic and the comic give them further affinities with the drama
of Chekhov, but in combining these features with a heightened
awareness of social etiquette and a wittiness of dialogue, they
reveal an important variation and extension of the comedy of
manners.

Orton

Joe Orton's tragically short career as a dramatist lasted for
only three years: the first production of *Entertaining Mr
Sloane* was in 1964; he was murdered in 1967. His inclusion in
this book is based on the three full-length stage works, *Entertaining Mr Sloane*, *Loot* (1965) and *What the Butler Saw* (first
produced in 1969): plays which become gradually more mannered and artificial as we move from the lower-middle-class
environment of Ed, Kath and Dada through the more sophisti-

cated world of Fay and Hal to the consulting room of Dr Prentice, which witnesses such strange variations on the sexual theme. This gradual upgrading of the social setting is matched by a concomitant development of style — in several senses of the word — so as to constitute for us a comprehensive study of the comedy of manners form. This awareness of the *mores* of different social classes is basic to Orton's moral and sexual satire, a feature to which he drew attention in the interview for the *Transatlantic Review* (1967):

> In actual fact the 'class' of my plays is going up all the time. *The Ruffian on the Stair* began by being pretty grotty and criminal; *Sloane* moved up slightly, since the characters were lower middle class. (Lower-middle-class nihilism, I was told.) *Loot* has moved up one rung more because it's now a woman who leaves £19,000 including her bonds and jewels. I'm sure you can — though I don't know that I can yet — write about very upper class people and make them as interesting as lower class people.

(*Behind the Scenes: Theatre and Film Interviews from the Transatlantic Review*, ed. Joseph F. McCrindle (New York, 1971), p. 118)

Not only does the social environment, and with it the style, change, but the basic dramatic structure of his plays develops as Orton moves further and further into the realms of farce. Moreover, as his desire to shock becomes more pronounced, the frenetic pace of his last play is matched by the ever-increasing allusions to sexual perversion and depravity. Much the most successful of the plays is *Loot* because the dramatic construction is so tight and because the work is more deeply and consistently shocking. The balance between humour and seriousness of satiric purpose is carefully calculated as the play grows into a rapidly deepening black farce. In his final — and probably unfinished — drama Orton's technique is at its most extreme, its most mannered, its most artificial, and the presentation of his 'very upper class people' less effective.

Sloane marked Orton's emergence as a dramatist, opening at the New Arts Theatre Club on May 6th 1964. It is important to stress that from the start Orton was considered a shocking and subversive writer, but the disturbing aspect of this early play resides as much in the language and style of the work as in violence of the action. As Taylor puts it:

> What is beautifully kept up in *Mr Sloane*, rather less so in his other plays, is the almost surrealistic dislocation between the most extraordinary and improper happenings and the unruffled propriety of the characters' conversation. The two elements are held in perfect balance . . . . the respectable-looking suburban household of middle-aged woman, doddering father and regularly visiting businessman brother into which he comes, so sure of himself, is, for all its façade of respectability, its refined speech and genteel manners, far more outrageous, far more dangerous, than anything Mr Sloane has in his silly little head. (*The Second Wave*, p. 129-30)

It is instructive to look more closely at this style, since Orton's aims in this play are rather different from those evident in the later dramas: a fact which Taylor misrepresents, and in consequence he does justice to neither *Loot* nor *What the Butler Saw*.

Kath's seduction of Sloane at the end of Act I is a perfect example of the way Orton's comic style works:

Kath: Isn't this room gorgeous?

Sloane: Yes.

Kath: That vase over there come from Bombay. Do you have any interest in that part of the world?

Sloane: I like Dieppe.

Kath: Ah . . . it's all the same. I don't suppose they know the difference themselves. Are you comfortable? Let me plump your cushion. (*She plumps a cushion behind his head. Laughs lightly.*) I really by rights should ask you to change places. This light is showing me up. (*Pause.*) I blame it on the manufacturers. They make garments so thin nowadays you'd think they intended to provoke a rape.

(*Entertaining Mr Sloane*, p. 41)

Whilst owing much to Pinter, the style of this passage recalls the Elyot—Amanda balcony scene in the first act of *Private Lives*. Once again there is a reluctance to speak about the real matter in hand as Kath hides behind the subterfuge of small talk. Her desire to impress both with the opulence of the room and her attempts at refined speech misfires with comic results. Sloane sees the picture clearly, but his comment: 'You're a teaser 'ent you?' is countered by Kath breaking away and saying 'I hope I'm not'. The adoption of conventional moral attitudes by Kath and Ed in the play is not a mere pose: they are both sincere, and though the audience is aware of the hypocrisy of their apparent double standards, they are not. This is a feature carried much further, and with even more success, in *Loot*: the sincerity and belief in their innocence is a characteristic of all Orton's villains, and it is by exposing the gap between their actions and their words that Orton moves into the realm of comedy of manners. As his plays develop they reveal a widening of that gap as speech, through wit and epigram, becomes more polished and refined. Orton cleverly reveals Ed's two-sided moral stance in Act III when Sloane turns to seduction to enlist his help. Far from being the empty-headed thug Taylor suggests, Sloane shrewdly realizes that to win he must play the game according to Ed's rules. He thus tells Ed the suggestive story of the man, 'an expert on the adolescent male body', who 'during the course of one magical night talked of his principles'. Sloane gradually adopts the evasions of style, the euphemisms and innuendoes he has heard those around him employ and in so doing wins Ed over to condoning his father's

murder. The final exchanges of the scene are a model of mannered comedy as Orton wittily captures the essence of this new
understanding in the relationship:

> *Sloane*: If you were to make the same demands I'd answer
>   loudly in the affirmative.
> *Ed*: You mean that?
> *Sloane*: In future you'd have nothing to complain of.
> *Ed*: You really mean what you say?
> *Sloane*: Let me live with you. I'd wear my jeans out in your
>   service. Cook for you.
> *Ed*: I eat out.
> *Sloane*: Bring you your tea in bed.
> *Ed*: Only women drink tea in bed.
> *Sloane*: You bring me my tea in bed then. Any arrangement
>   you fancy.
>
> (*Ibid*, p. 83)

Such a conversation is all the more striking and disturbing
after the violence we have witnessed, but it is entirely sympto-
matic of the way Orton was to develop dramatically, in that
physical violence more and more gives way to the cut and
thrust of wit and repartee. We get a further glimpse of this at
the end of *Sloane* when Ed, determined to get Sloane away
from Kath, turns violent; but the violence is expressed through
a virulence of language, hardly witty at this point, but very
funny as Ed's mounting anger finds increasingly more outrageous insults to heap on his sister:

> *Ed*: Look in the glass, lady. Let's enjoy a laugh. (*He takes
>   her to the mirror.*) What do you see?
> *Kath*: Me.
> *Ed*: What are you?
> *Kath*: My hair is nice. Natural. I'm mature, but still able to
>   command a certain appeal.
> *Ed*: You look like death! Flabby mouth. Wrinkled neck.
>   Puffy hands.

Kath: It's baby coming.
Ed: Sagging tits. You cradle-snatcher.
Kath: He said I was a Venus. I held him in my arms.
Ed: What a martyrdom!

(Ibid, p. 90)

After the euphemistic conversation with Sloane, Ed's insistence here on calling a spade a spade is doubly ironic, the more so as Kath vies with him in her desperate attempt to draw a verbal veil over her physical appearance. The linguistic force is sharpened even more finely at the end of the play when Ed and Kath come to their own private arrangement regarding Sloane's future. The struggle for sexual dominance and possession — a basic theme of comedy of manners — is here resolved in this image of a double wedding, though to expand this into a conscious wedding service (as the film, released in 1970, did) is to coarsen the wit in Orton's dénouement and to misinterpret the basic sense of decorum which prevails right to the end.

Loot, Orton's second full-length play, is even more at pains to shock, but achieves its effects by the most careful means. Again the major characters operate on a series of moral equivocations, but here the gap between the two codes is very much wider. Fay is rigid in matters of social decorum and a blindly pious Catholic, but she has murdered all her previous employers for their money, Mrs McLeavy being the eighth. Again it is vital to stress the lack of conscious hypocrisy, most emphatically evident in her (very Catholic) confession when she is caught.

Hal and Dennis are bank robbers and homosexual lovers, but they are both saddled with Dennis's infantile devotion to Fay and Hal's absolute inability to lie. Orton extracts a great deal of comedy from the juxtaposition of these different moral standards, which the characters see as being in no sense incompatible. When Dennis urges Hal to lie the latter answers truthfully: 'I can't, baby, it's my upbringing', which leads to the brilliant confrontation between Hal and Truscott, the police inspector, where Orton exploits the inexorable logic of the situation to the full:

Truscott: Why do you make such stupid remarks?

Hal: I'm a stupid person. That's what I'm trying to say.

Truscott: What proof have I that you're stupid? Give me an example of your stupidity.

Hal: I can't.

Truscott: Why not? I don't believe you're stupid at all.

Hal: I am. I had a hand in the bank job.

> Fay *draws a sharp breath*. Hal *sits frozen*. Truscott *takes his pipe from his mouth*.
>
> (*with a nervous laugh*) There, that's stupid, isn't it? Telling you that.

Truscott: (*also laughing*) You must be stupid if you expect me to believe you. Why, if you had a hand in the bank job, you wouldn't tell me.

Fay: Not unless he was stupid.

(*Loot*, p. 45)

It is the inverted comic logic of *Loot* which is the play's most outstanding feature, carried to its ultimate in Truscott's disguise. He gains entrance to the house by masquerading as a Water Board Inspector since he has no search warrant, but his every action is that of a policeman. Hence Orton can satirize the misplaced trust which the characters — and notably McLeavy — place in authority, a trust which is shown up in Truscott's revelation of his true nature when he finally arrests Fay. Here Truscott's witty countering of her objections is more genuinely shocking than anything in *Sloane*, as the author's own mistrust of the police is given a very sharp cutting edge:

Fay: I'm innocent until I'm proved guilty.

Truscott: Who's been filling your head with that rubbish?

Fay: I can't be had for anything. You've no proof.

Truscott: When I make out my report I shall say that you've

given me a confession. It could prejudice your case if I
have to forge one.

Fay: I shall deny that I've confessed.

Truscott: Perjury is a serious crime.

Fay: Have you no respect for the truth?

Truscott: We have a saying under the blue lamp: 'Waste
time on the truth and you'll be pounding the beat until
the day you retire.'

Fay: The British police force used to be run by men of
integrity.

Truscott: That is a mistake which has been rectified.

(*Ibid*, pp. 66-7)

The play traces the shifting of the money from the wardrobe to
Mrs McLeavy's coffin, then back to the house; and the parallel
progress of Mrs McLeavy's embalmed body from coffin to
wardrobe to garage as Hal and Dennis are forced to include
first Fay and then Truscott in their sharing of the loot. Sexual
conflicts are present but here the overriding drive is that other
essential motivation in comedy of manners: money. The
unscrupulous dénouement might be from Wycherley, as the
blame is put on the innocent party, McLeavy, so that the other
three may share the spoils.

The development of the action throughout is absolutely
clear, totally inevitable (given the dual values which play havoc
with everyone's schemes) and yet constantly subject to twists
and surprises as characters stumble on secrets and attempt to
unravel the truth. The play, in fact, adheres to all the rules of
perfect farce. Orton has expressed his admiration for Ben Travers in particular, his own title being an acknowledgement of his
debt to Travers' *Plunder*. But whereas popular English farce in
the tradition of Pinero (both the Aldwych and the Whitehall
varieties) rests on accepted conventions of behaviour which
only *appear* to have been disregarded, in *Loot* the conventions
have been flung aside. In a conventional modern farce the

humour arises because an innocent party appears to be an adulterer or a pervert; in *Loot* the catalogue of unconventional behaviour ranges from homosexuality to murder and theft. Hence the rigorous moral standards to which Orton's characters cling should not be misinterpreted: Orton's topsy-turvy logic is more disturbing, but it is no less inflexible and acts as the foundation on which the satire in his comedy of manners is built. Entirely characteristic is Truscott's moral stance when he says that he believes Fay to be guilty of another crime 'which the law regards as far more serious than the taking of human life' — namely 'stealing public money'. The apparently farcical inversion of values, owing a great deal to Gilbert and Wilde, points in fact to a more disturbing truth.

When asked in the *Transatlantic Review* interview if he had an ultimate aim as a playwright, Orton replied: 'I'd like to write a play as good as *The Importance of Being Earnest*' and added, ironically, of Wilde: 'I admire his work, not his life. It was an appalling life'. This indebtedness to Wilde is to be found not only in the construction of the play as a whole, but in the heightened tone of the language throughout. The sharper, more epigrammatic quality evident in this play befits the move up the social scale as well as the fact that Hal, Fay and Truscott are much cleverer than the others, or indeed than any character in *Sloane*. It is significant that the sustained passages of witty conversation are limited to these three, by far the most sophisticated figures in the play. An example is Fay's attack on Hal where we see him fully capable of countering the tartness of her moral objections:

Fay: (*Folding her hands in her lap.*) The priest at St Kilda's
    has asked me to speak to you. He's very worried. He says
    you spend your time thieving from slot machines and
    deflowering the daughters of better men than yourself. Is
    this a fact?
Hal: Yes.

Fay: And even the sex you were born into isn't safe from your marauding. Father Mac is popular for the remission of sins, as you know. But clearing up after you is a full-time job. He simply cannot be in the confessional twenty-four hours a day. That's reasonable isn't it? You do see his point.

Hal: Yes.

Fay: What are you going to do about this dreadful state of affairs?

Hal: I'm going abroad.

Fay: That will please the fathers. Who are you going with?

Hal: A mate of mine, Dennis. A very luxurious type of lad. At present employed by an undertaker. And doing well in the profession.

Fay: Have you known him long?

Hal: We shared the same cradle.

Fay: Was that economy or malpractice?

Hal: We were too young then to practice, and economics still defeat us.

(*Ibid*, pp. 11-12)

This is comedy of manners in its most complete Wildean sense. There is a perfect precision in the choice of cutting words — 'marauding' and 'luxurious', for example — and throughout the intellectual cleverness is related to the emotional situation of the characters. There is a healthy sexual rivalry underpinning this exchange which in this respect recalls the 'tea' scene between Gwendolen and Cecily in *The Importance*. Orton sticks to his own rules here in that the conversation is regulated by Fay's equivocal moral standards as well as by Hal's inability to lie, and yet the inner logic of the scene does not preclude the aiming of a variety of satiric darts at social and religious institutions.

The opening conversation between Dr Prentice and Geraldine in *What the Butler Saw* is also indicative of Orton's desire in this final play to write in the artificial manner of Wilde. It illustrates the basic difficulties presented by the employment of a further extreme of style in this piece.

> *Prentice*: Who was your father? Put that at the head of the page. (Geraldine *puts the cardboard box she is carrying to one side, crosses her legs, rests the notebook upon her knee and makes a note.*) And now the reply immediately underneath for quick reference.
>
> *Geraldine*: I've no idea who my father was. (Dr Prentice *is perturbed by her reply although he gives no evidence of this. He gives her a kindly smile.*)
>
> *Prentice*: I'd better be frank, Miss Barkley. I can't employ you if you're in any way miraculous. It would be contrary to established practice. You did have a father?
>
> *Geraldine*: Oh, I'm sure I did. My mother was frugal in her habits, but she'd never economize unwisely.
>
> (*What the Butler Saw*, pp. 7-8)

The echoes here of the interrogation scene in *The Importance* are too loud, coming at the very opening of the play; but the real problem is that Orton has allowed his desire to write funny dialogue to overrule any consideration of true characterization. Wilde was shrewd enough to offset Lady Bracknell's acerbity and outraged propriety against Jack's simplicity of manner, but here Orton makes Geraldine every bit as witty a figure as Prentice, most notably in the phrasing of her last reply quoted above. Later in the play Geraldine emerges as a naive figure, the rather dim secretary who is the straight character around whom the escalating farce of the play revolves; in this opening scene the audience is given quite the wrong impression — a crucial miscalculation on Orton's part. What Stephen Sondheim has to say about a parallel lack of artistic consideration in his composition of the lyrics for *West Side Story* is instructive:

I had spent the previous year of my life rhyming 'day' and 'way' and 'me' and 'be' and with 'I feel pretty'. I wanted to show that I could do inner rhymes too. So I had this uneducated Puerto Rican girl singing 'It's alarming how charming I feel'. You know she would not have been unwelcome in Noel Coward's living room ... When rhyme goes against character, out it should go, and rhyme always implies education and mind-working, and the more rhymes the sharper the mind.

(Quoted in Craig Zadan, *Sondheim and Co.* (New York, 1974), p. 23).

The same holds true of wit, and such is the delicate balance of comedy of manners that the dramatist cannot afford to dispense with this vital consideration.

What the Butler Saw was dismissed by most critics, including John Russell Taylor whose approach is extreme:

It tries to work like *Loot*, only this time guying the conventions of farce instead of the whodunnit. But to burlesque something which depends from the beginning on its quality of burlesque is almost a logical impossibility: if you parody a parody where do you end up if not back where you started? ... there is a bad technical error involved: to make comedy out of the extraordinary, a play needs a norm, and farce above all needs its straight man. (*The Second Wave*, pp. 137-8)

Geraldine is the norm in the play; the 'bad technical error' resides only in Orton's initial presentation of her, for if we look carefully we can see a basic logic and a psychological truth underlying the actions of all the characters. This is the case with Dr Prentice and his wife whose relationship, contrary to Taylor's analysis, is credibly and carefully presented by Orton. There is a good deal of what Coward (in the Preface to *Private Lives*) calls 'sound sex psychology' underlying their marital quarrels. Take this, for example:

Mrs Prentice *gives a nervy toss of her head and drinks whisky.*

Prentice: She's an example of in-breeding among the lobelia-growing classes. A failure in eugenics, combined with a taste for alcohol and sexual intercourse, makes it undesirable for her to become a mother.

Mrs Prentice: (*quietly*) I hardly ever have sexual intercourse.

Prentice: You were born with your legs apart. They'll send you to the grave in a Y-shaped coffin.

Mrs Prentice: (*with a brittle laugh*) My trouble stems from your inadequacy as a lover! It's embarrassing. You must have learned your technique from a Christmas cracker. (*Her mouth twists into a sneer.*) Rejuvenation pills have no effect on you.

Prentice: (*stuffily*) I never take pills.

Mrs Prentice: You take them all the time during our love-making. The deafening sound of your chewing is the reason for my never having an orgasm.

(*What the Butler Saw*, p. 15)

Though the mannered style of this exchange is extreme we should not doubt that the repartee is an intellectual extension of the vehemence of feeling: the two are fighting much as George and Martha do in *Who's Afraid of Virginia Woolf?* and they, too, need a third party, indeed an ex-lover, as audience. When Dr Rance arrives, however, it rapidly becomes clear that his mental agility is employed for verbal effect rather than to achieve any concrete aim. The actor playing Rance is faced with a far more difficult problem in making the character believable, and this difficulty increases as Rance attempts to formulate an analysis of the rapidly developing state of affairs by expanding his own demented thesis. Unlike the characters in *Loot* the figures in this play have very negative responses which govern their actions; instead of being motivated by any

clear objectives, they are concerned either to avoid a confrontation with reality or to solve the paradoxes of the situation. The
clear-cut and direct motivations of sex and money give way
here to something more nebulous. At the end of the play Geraldine says: 'The whole day has been spent fighting to retain my
self respect' — a very difficult line of action for an actress to put
across to an audience.

The farcical situation escalates on a par with the stylization
of the language. Orton brilliantly exploits the potential of
disguise, mistaken identity and misunderstanding in the
cleverly-timed entrances of a small group of characters. And
he uses the paraphernalia of farce to shock. When Sergeant
Match first arrives, Nick is compelled to take Dr Prentice's
advice and disguise himself as a girl. At this precise moment
Mrs Prentice enters and catches him with his trousers down in
the company of her husband. Her sense of outrage goes far
beyond what the conventions of farce would lead us to expect,
but Orton can go further. When Dr Rance cross-questions the
disguised Nick he mistakenly assumes he is a girl and the
disguised Geraldine is a boy. This results in him saying, in
answer to Nick's question 'What is unnatural?':

> *Rance*: (*to* Nick) Suppose I made an indecent suggestion to
> you? If you agreed something might occur which, by and
> large, would be regarded as natural. If, on the other
> hand, I approached this child — (*he smiles at* Geraldine)
> — my action could result only in a gross violation of the
> order of things.
>
> (*Ibid*, p. 60)

This is Orton the sexual rebel, employing farce to disturb his
audience's conventional moral response. He is equally skilful
in employing the witty dialogue of comedy of manners to
exactly the same end elsewhere as the apparently superficial
brilliance of Rance's responses serves a more serious ironic purpose:

> *Rance*: Perhaps this accusation springs from disappointment. It might have been wiser if you hadn't rejected the young fellow's blandishments.
>
> *Prentice*: Unnatural vice can ruin a man.
>
> *Rance*: Ruin follows the accusation, not the vice. Had you committed the act you would not now be facing the charge.
>
> *Prentice*: I couldn't commit the act. I'm a heterosexual.
>
> *Rance*: I wish you wouldn't use these Chaucerian words.
>
> (Ibid, p. 55)

At this point in the play we feel that Orton is in complete control: situation and language interact to very subtle effect. Undeniably he allows the action later to become too mechanical; the more it becomes separated from character and the interplay of personal relationships the less effective is his ability to shock by making us believe in the characters and circumstances. The dénouement is characteristic: a parody of *The Importance of Being Earnest* gives way to the discovery of the penis from Churchill's statue — a twist of the plot which has little effect because, unlike the surprising revelations in *Loot*, we have not been adequately prepared for it; Geraldine brought on the vital box at the start of the play and it has not been referred to since. The final line of the play and the stage directions which follow:

> *Rance*: I'm glad you don't despise tradition. Let us put our clothes on and face the world.
>
> (*They pick up their clothes and weary, bleeding, drugged and drunk, climb the rope-ladder into the blazing light.*)
>
> (Ibid, p. 92)

hint at a deeper level of seriousness which is evident in several parts of the work and which might have emerged more clearly throughout had Orton lived to revise it. As it stands we should appreciate the fusion in his work of the comedy of manners with the contrasted genres of farce and situation comedy, resulting in a highly original and powerfully subversive drama.

5
Conclusion

Our countrymen . . . are more cunning than practical. When they make
up their ledger, they balance stupidity by wealth, and vice by hypocrisy.
(Oscar Wilde, *The Picture of Dorian Gray*, 1891).

This study has analysed the continuity of an essentially English
dramatic tradition with particular reference to two centuries:
the seventeenth and the twentieth. By the end of the nineteenth
century the comedy of manners had fallen into such disrepute
that Meredith could dismiss it as unworthy of serious consideration. He saw the post-Restoration drama in England as
divorced from the major European comic tradition and disap-
proved of it. His definition, however, holds good in its reference to 'comedy of the manners of South Sea islanders under
city veneer'. Meredith observed in the drama of the late seventeenth century a savagery of motive beneath the glittering surface of a decorous and witty style. For him this savagery
resided in the search for sexual satisfaction, though in fact the
characters are equally unscrupulous both in their pursuit of a
fortune and in their betrayal of friendship. It is this mercenary
opportunism which is such a distinctive mark of English social
comedy: in *Man and Superman* when Violet remarks: 'You
can be as romantic as you please about love, Hector; but you
mustn't be romantic about money', her American husband
replies: 'That's very English' (p. 64).

It was Wilde, a contemporary of Meredith and Shaw, who
was to satirize the hypocrisy of his own age by exploring the

dichotomy between word and deed. Fundamental to his plays — as to those of the late seventeenth century — is the vigorous rejection of Puritan values. His command of language and his ironic exposé of the manners of society was a return to the form and subject of post-Restoration comedy which has resulted in the immense popularity of the genre in the present century. Through the refining influence of Coward, who crystallized the particular strength of English understatement in the brief exchanges so characteristic of his dialogue, a brand of drama has re-emerged which is acutely concerned with the *mores* of social living. This comedy of manners, like that of Wycherley or Congreve, deals with the rational organization of man's most basic drives, while it is precisely the contrast between the coolness of technique and the passionate or sordid nature of these human motives which gives the plays their sharply ironic perspective. Wilde, moreover, was the first of several homosexual writers in England who used social comedy to reveal the nature of sexual hypocrisy. Though in his plays he confined himself to heterosexual subjects, the conflict between his own private life and his public image made itself felt in the outrageousness both of his social *persona* and his literary style. The sexual outsider may very well feel an affinity with this comic genre which consistently reveals the hollowness of conventional moral pretensions, though it is only in the work of Orton that we see the full potential of this aspect explored. Coward, like Wilde, assiduously cultivated a brilliant public image, and the sharpness resulting from their detachment as well as the subversive quality of both these writers has undoubtedly left its mark on those playwrights, notably Osborne and Pinter, who have been influenced by them.

The fundamentally English nature of this comic genre is revealed all the more clearly by an examination of the plays of Edward Albee which, because they possess many features of this dramatic convention, are worthy of more detailed discussion here. Like Pinter, Albee has developed from the absurdist vein of such early comedies of menace as *The Zoo Story* (1958) to a wittier, more sophisticated, social comedy. *All Over* (1971) is his most tightly-structured, rigorously controlled essay in this genre to date, and it is interesting that it should have received praise from Pinter who has said: '*All Over* is a most rich, quite remarkable achievement. I feel it to be a major work and something that has made a great impact on me' (Quoted on the dust-jacket of the English edn.) Albee also resembles Pinter in the dramatization of the relentless games his characters play. In *Who's Afraid of Virginia Woolf?* (1962) the marriage is kept alive by a ritual more vicious and savage than that in *The Lover*, but there is a parallel between the invented lover of the one and the invented child of the other as well as a marked similarity in the way the husband in each case takes the initiative and forces the wife to face the sexual issues more directly: George, like Richard, pushes the logic of this game to its ultimate conclusion as well as involving the guests in others, from Humiliate the Host through Get the Guest to Hump the Hostess. Though the guests are not playing games of this sort in *A Delicate Balance* (1966) everyone is subjected to the rules of the house as laid down by Agnes, whilst a ritual of a different sort governs the actions of the characters in *All Over*. Propriety and form are all important: Agnes confesses to being 'a stickler on points of manners, timing, tact, the graces'; and in *All Over* The Wife explains the presence of The Mistress at her husband's death bed thus: 'It is more or less required that you be ... I think here. Isn't it one of our customs?'

In each of these three dramas the more highly articulate characters manipulate the others, mocking their inability to cope with their feelings, and from one play to the next we observe a refinement of verbal conflict so that the rawness of *Who's Afraid of Virginia Woolf* develops through the subtler language of *A Delicate Balance* to the complexity of *All Over*, which opens with a pointed and clever semantic argument. Agnes is scathing about the messiness she observes in the lives of her sister and daughter; in *All Over* it is The Mistress who draws attention to the more disturbing linguistic impoverishment consequent upon such emotional and verbal carelessness:

> You lash out — which can be a virtue, I dare say, stridency aside, if it's used to protect and not just as a revenge . . . but you're careless, not only with facts, but of *yourself*. What words will you have left if you use them all to kill? (*All Over*, p. 64)

In all three of these plays, however, the mask of decorum, of games playing, of social ritual, finally crumbles. Martha confesses that she is afraid of Virginia Woolf: she is frightened of facing life without the comforting evasions of the complex marital game. It is Tobias who breaks down at the end of *A Delicate Balance*, realizing that the demands made by his friends (who in a very Pinteresque way dispossess him, and then his daughter, of their rooms) have proved him lacking. At the climax of *All Over* the reality of death forces The Wife to utter the great cry 'that has been pent up for thirty years' and which 'finally explodes from her'. Yet within a few moments she has regained control and the play ends with The Doctor's elliptical utterance 'all over': a movement which matches the delicate balance established at the close of the previous drama as well as the inexorable conclusion of 'The Exorcism' comprising the third part of *Who's Afraid of Virginia Woolf?*

Nowhere does Albee more closely resemble Pinter than in the way in which he allows lengthy anecdotes to surface amidst terse snatches of conversation, thus producing a strange dislocating effect. Notable are George's tale of the young boy asking for 'bergin', Tobias's story of the cat and The Friend's account of his meeting with his insane wife. Albee's employment of these anecdotes, however, lacks the ambiguity of Pinter who questions the authenticity of the narratives as well as allowing his characters — notably in *Old Times* — to take one another up on these issues later. In Albee's plays these accounts have the force of confessions, directly expressive of the characters' fears and guilt. In causing them to bare their souls in this way he reveals himself to be firmly in the dramatic tradition of Eugene O'Neill.

Even more revealing is the approach to money in his plays. Albee is not concerned with the unscrupulous financial acquisitiveness so basic to the English comedy of manners; his characters are all wealthy, even The Mistress in *All Over*, who is quick to point out the nature of her motives:

> I'm not an intruder in the dollar sense. I've more than enough — I was born with it. Don't you people ever take the trouble to scout? And I told your father I wanted nothing beyond his company . . . and love . . . So I am not your platinum blonde with the chewing gum and the sequined dress. (*Ibid*, p. 70)

When Martha taunts George for only earning an associate professor's salary she points up the crucial American emphasis. Albee is concerned to attack not hypocrisy in monetary matters but the falseness of the idealism associated with the American Dream. Nick embodies these qualities (as does the central character of Albee's play *The American Dream* (1961)), and it is the handling of this success ethic, with all its psychological and sexual implications, which accounts for the major difference between Albee's social comedies and those of his English contemporaries. The puritan tradition in America, with its insistence on the virtue of work and the belief in an equality of opportunity for all, has left a further mark: essentially America is a classless society. George and Nick struggle as social equals despite their different backgrounds, and though Martha and George may be worse hosts than Agnes and Tobias there is no class distinction involved in the comparison. It is the absence of social snobbery along with the relative lack of concern with money that sets Albee's plays firmly apart from the English tradition.

An awareness of class is basic to all English comedy of manners — by class being understood both social rank and breeding. We have seen how this genre, at first given an essentially aristocratic setting, has now developed to encompass all areas of society. Since Coward a middle-class milieu has predominated and now we may observe, notably in the plays of Pinter and Orton, a dramatization of class conflict and an observation of the niceties of bourgeois behaviour which replace the clash of urban and rural values in the plays of the post-Restoration period. In exploring the implications of its initial definition this study has emphasized throughout the significance of breeding; breeding as defined by style, by the image we present to the world, the way we behave, ultimately our choice of dress or speech. It expresses itself in something as apparently insignificant as the choice of a necktie as well as in the life-time organization of an emotional and intellectual code of behaviour.

Comedy of manners, then, examines in detail the behaviour and conventions of civilized society. Financial and sexual success are seen as determining the conduct of a group of characters bound together through ties of friendship and marriage. There is a fundamental concern with style and breeding, a desire to formulate — in Coward's phrase — a design for living. Since this brand of comedy has achieved its richest expression in two periods, the post-Restoration and the modern, it is ultimately to five plays we must turn in order to appreciate the full potential of this dramatic genre: namely, *The Way of the World*, *The Importance of Being Earnest*, *Design For Living*, *Loot* and *The Homecoming*. These plays will no doubt continue to enjoy successful theatrical revival, for they are the finest examples of our most important native comic tradition.

Bibliography and further reading

Wherever possible quotations from seventeenth- and eighteenth-century plays are taken from the four-volume *Restoration Comedy*, edited by A. Norman Jeffares (London and Totowa, New Jersey, 1974).

Plays not included in the above collection are referred to in the following: *The Comedies of William Congreve*, edited with an introduction by Norman Marshall (London, 1948); *John Dryden*, edited with an introduction and notes by George Saintsbury in the Mermaid Series, two volumes (London, n.d.); *The Plays of Richard Brinsley Sheridan*, edited with an introduction by Iolo A. Williams (London, 1926); *William Wycherley*, edited with an introduction and notes by A.C. Ward, in the Mermaid Series (London, n.d.).

Steele's *The Tender Husband* is in *Bell's British Theatre*, Vol. 8 (London, 1778); Bickerstaff's *The Plain Dealer* in *Bell's British Theatre*, Vol. 31 (London, 1796); Garrick's *The Country Girl* in the edition with remarks by Mrs Inchbald (London, 1806), and Gilbert's *Engaged* in *The Magistrate and Other Nineteenth-Century Plays*, edited by Michael Booth (Oxford, 1974). The plays of Wilde are quoted from the Penguin edition (Harmondsworth, 1954).

Plays of the inter-war period are to be found in the following editions: *The Last of Mrs Cheyney* by Frederick Lonsdale (London, 1925) published by Collins; *The Collected Plays of W. Somerset Maugham* (London, 1931), *Play Parade Vol. 1* by Noel Coward (London, 1934) and *Tonight at 8.30* by Noel

Coward (London, 1936), published by Heinemann. The plays of Orton and Pinter are published by Eyre Methuen; those of Osborne by Faber & Faber; and those of Albee by Jonathan Cape.

The following books are suggested as a basis for further reading

Brown, J.R. and Harris, B. (eds), *Restoration Theatre* (London, 1965).

Dobrée, B., *Restoration Comedy* (Oxford, 1924).

Lamb, C., *The Essays of Elia*, in the Everyman's Library edition (London, 1906).

Loftis, J. (ed.), *Restoration Drama, Modern Essays in Criticism* (New York, 1966).

Macaulay, T.B., *Critical and Historical Essays*, in the Everyman's Library edition (London, 1907).

Meredith, G., *An Essay on the Idea of Comedy and of the Uses of the Comic Spirit,* in the Standard edition (London, 1919).

Morley, S., *A Talent to Amuse* (London, 1969).

Muir, K., *The Comedy of Manners* (London, 1970).

Sawyer, W.S., *The Comedy of Manners from Sheridan to Maugham* (New York, 1961).

Taylor, J.R., *The Rise and Fall of the Well-Made Play* (London, 1967).

Taylor, J.R., *The Second Wave* (London, 1971).

Index